CYBERSECURITY FUNDAMENTALS

A Comprehensive Guide on The Basics of Cybersecurity, including Threat Detection, Prevention Techniques, and Best Practices

BY

LIM GUAN LENG

TABLE OF CONTENTS

INTRODUCTION

In an era defined by rapid technological advancements and an everincreasing reliance on digital infrastructure, cybersecurity has emerged as a paramount concern. The digital revolution has brought about unprecedented convenience and connectivity, transforming the way we live, work, and communicate. However, this transformation has also given rise to a host of cyber threats that have the potential to disrupt lives, businesses, and entire nations.

Cybersecurity is the practice of protecting systems, networks, and programs from digital attacks. These attacks are usually aimed at accessing, changing, or destroying sensitive information, extorting money from users, or interrupting normal business processes. The significance of cybersecurity cannot be overstated as our world becomes more interconnected and dependent on digital technologies. At its core, cybersecurity encompasses a range of practices, technologies, and processes designed to safeguard computer systems, networks, and data from unauthorized access or damage. It involves everything from securing personal devices and home networks to protecting complex corporate infrastructures and national critical systems. The scope of cybersecurity extends across various domains, including information security, network security, application security, and operational security, among others.

The concept of cybersecurity has evolved significantly since the inception of the internet. In the early days, cybersecurity was primarily focused on protecting mainframe computers and rudimentary networks. As the internet expanded and became integral to daily life, the nature of cyber threats evolved, becoming more sophisticated and widespread. The advent of e-commerce, social media, cloud computing, and the Internet of Things (IoT) has further complicated the cybersecurity landscape, necessitating more advanced and comprehensive security measures.

Today, cybersecurity is more relevant than ever. Cyber threats are no longer confined to the realm of science fiction; they are a real and present danger that can affect anyone, from individuals and small businesses to large corporations and government entities. High-profile cyber attacks have made headlines worldwide, underscoring the vulnerabilities that exist in our digital infrastructure and the devastating consequences of security breaches.

The rise of ransom ware attacks, data breaches, and cyber espionage has highlighted the need for robust cybersecurity measures. Personal data, intellectual property, financial information, and even national security are at risk. The proliferation of connected devices and the increasing complexity of cyber threats mean that cybersecurity is a constantly evolving field that requires ongoing vigilance and adaptation. In modern society, cybersecurity plays a critical role in maintaining trust and confidence in the digital ecosystem. It ensures the confidentiality, integrity, and availability of data, which are essential for the smooth operation of businesses, government functions, and daily life. Effective cybersecurity measures protect against financial losses, reputational damage, and legal repercussions, providing a foundation for innovation and growth in the digital age.

Moreover, cybersecurity is not just a technical issue; it is a societal one. It involves ethical considerations, legal frameworks, and international cooperation. As cyber threats continue to evolve, the need for a collective and coordinated approach to cybersecurity becomes increasingly apparent. This involves not only technical solutions but also education, awareness, and the development of a cybersecurity culture. This book, "Cybersecurity Fundamentals: A Comprehensive Guide on the Basics of Cybersecurity, Including Threat Detection, Prevention Techniques, and Best Practices," aims to provide a thorough and accessible introduction to the field of cybersecurity. Whether you are a novice seeking to understand the basics or a professional looking to deepen your knowledge, this book offers valuable insights into the core principles and practices of cybersecurity.

By exploring various types of cyber threats, detection methods, prevention techniques, and best practices, this book will equip you with the knowledge needed to navigate the complex and ever-changing cybersecurity landscape. Each chapter delves into a specific aspect of cybersecurity, providing detailed explanations, real-world examples, and practical advice.

As you embark on this journey through the world of cybersecurity, you will gain a deeper understanding of the challenges and opportunities that lie ahead. You will learn how to protect yourself and your organization from cyber threats, respond effectively to incidents, and contribute to a safer and more secure digital environment.

Welcome to the world of cybersecurity. Let's begin this journey together.

CHAPTER **1**

UNDERSTANDING CYBERSECURITY

Cybersecurity is a critical aspect of our digital world, focusing on the protection of computer systems, networks, and data from malicious attacks. Its significance has grown alongside the advancement of technology, as our dependence on digital infrastructure continues to expand. Cybersecurity encompasses a broad range of practices and measures designed to prevent unauthorized access, data breaches, and other cyber threats. As we delve into the history and evolution of cybersecurity, it becomes clear how this field has developed in response to the ever-changing landscape of digital threats.

The roots of cybersecurity can be traced back to the early days of computing, when the primary focus was on securing mainframe computers. These early systems were relatively isolated, and security measures were rudimentary, focusing mainly on physical access control.

As computer networks began to emerge, the need for more sophisticated security measures became apparent. The development of the ARPANET, the precursor to the modern internet, marked a significant milestone, introducing new challenges related to network security and data protection.

The 1980s and 1990s witnessed a rapid expansion of the internet, leading to an increase in cyber threats. The introduction of personal computers and the growth of online services created new opportunities for cybercriminals. During this period, notable incidents such as the Morris Worm in 1988 and the rise of computer viruses highlighted the vulnerabilities of digital systems. These events spurred the development of antivirus software and firewalls, marking the beginning of a more proactive approach to cybersecurity.

The early 2000s saw a proliferation of sophisticated cyber attacks, including phishing, denial-of-service (DoS) attacks, and data breaches. The rise of e-commerce and online banking brought about new security challenges, as cybercriminals targeted financial transactions and personal information. Governments and organizations began to recognize the importance of cybersecurity, leading to the establishment of regulatory frameworks and standards. This era also saw the emergence of cybersecurity as a professional field, with dedicated roles and specialized training programs.

Today, cybersecurity is a dynamic and rapidly evolving field, driven by the continuous advancement of technology and the increasing complexity of cyber threats. The rise of cloud computing, mobile devices, and the Internet of Things (IoT) has expanded the attack surface, necessitating more comprehensive and adaptive security measures. The advent of artificial intelligence (AI) and machine learning has also introduced new possibilities for both cyber defense and cyber offense. As we look to the future, the evolution of cybersecurity will undoubtedly continue, shaped by emerging technologies and the ongoing battle between defenders and attackers.

1.1. Fundamentals of Cybersecurity

The fundamentals of cybersecurity revolve around the principles and practices necessary to protect information systems from cyber threats. At its core, cybersecurity aims to ensure the confidentiality, integrity, and availability of data. Confidentiality involves protecting sensitive information from unauthorized access, ensuring that only authorized individuals can view or use the data. Integrity focuses on maintaining the accuracy and completeness of data, preventing unauthorized modifications. Availability ensures that information and resources are accessible to authorized users when needed, preventing disruptions to services.

One of the key components of cybersecurity is risk management, which involves identifying, assessing, and mitigating potential risks to information systems. This process begins with a thorough understanding of the threats and vulnerabilities that could impact an organization. Threats can come from various sources, including cybercriminals, insider threats, and natural disasters. Vulnerabilities are weaknesses in systems or processes that could be exploited by threats. By assessing the likelihood and potential impact of these risks, organizations can prioritize their security efforts and allocate resources effectively.

Another fundamental aspect of cybersecurity is the implementation of security controls. These controls are measures designed to reduce the risk of cyber threats and protect information systems. Security controls can be categorized into three types: preventive, detective, and corrective. Preventive controls aim to stop attacks before they occur, such as firewalls and access controls. Detective controls focus on identifying and monitoring potential security incidents, like intrusion detection systems and security information and event management (SIEM) solutions. Corrective controls are implemented to respond to and recover from security incidents, including backup and recovery processes and incident response plans.

A crucial element of cybersecurity is user education and awareness. Human error is often a significant factor in security breaches, making it essential to educate users about safe practices and potential threats. Training programs can help employees recognize phishing attempts, use strong passwords, and follow best practices for data protection. By fostering a culture of cybersecurity awareness, organizations can reduce the risk of human-related security incidents and enhance their overall security posture.

What is Cybersecurity?

Cybersecurity is the practice of protecting computer systems, networks, and data from unauthorized access, theft, damage, and other cyber threats. It involves a range of strategies and technologies designed to safeguard digital assets against cyber attacks. In today's interconnected world, cybersecurity is essential for individuals, businesses, and governments to protect sensitive information and ensure the reliable functioning of digital infrastructure. Cybersecurity encompasses everything from securing personal devices to protecting complex corporate networks and national critical systems.

The scope of cybersecurity extends across various domains, including information security, network security, application security, and operational security. Information security focuses on protecting data from unauthorized access and ensuring its confidentiality, integrity, and availability. Network security involves securing the communication channels and infrastructure that connect devices and systems, preventing unauthorized access and attacks. Application security focuses on protecting software applications from vulnerabilities and ensuring their secure development and deployment. Operational security encompasses the processes and procedures for managing and protecting information systems, including incident response and disaster recovery.

Cybersecurity is not just a technical issue but also involves human, organizational, and legal aspects. Effective cybersecurity requires a holistic approach that combines technological solutions with policies, procedures, and user awareness. It involves understanding the threat landscape, implementing appropriate security controls, and continuously monitoring and improving security measures. As cyber threats continue to evolve, the field of cybersecurity must adapt and innovate to stay ahead of potential attackers and protect our digital world.

Key Concepts and Terminology

Understanding the key concepts and terminology in cybersecurity is essential for grasping the fundamentals of the field. One of the core concepts is **confidentiality**, which ensures that sensitive information is only accessible to authorized individuals. Confidentiality is often achieved through encryption, access controls, and other security measures that restrict access to data. **Integrity** is another critical concept, focusing on maintaining the accuracy and consistency of data over its life-cycle. Integrity measures, such as checksums and digital signatures, help detect and prevent unauthorized modifications to data. **Availability** is a key concept that ensures information and resources are accessible to authorized users when needed. Availability is crucial for maintaining the functionality of systems and services, and it involves implementing measures such as redundancy, load balancing, and backup solutions to prevent disruptions. **Authentication** and **authorization** are also fundamental concepts in cybersecurity. Authentication verifies the identity of users or devices, typically through passwords, biometrics, or multi-factor authentication. Authorization determines the permissions and access levels granted to authenticated users, ensuring they can only access resources they are entitled to.

Another important concept is **risk management,** which involves identifying, assessing, and mitigating risks to information systems. Risk management helps organizations prioritize their security efforts and allocate resources effectively. **Threats, vulnerabilities, and exploits** are key terms related to risk management. Threats are potential dangers that can exploit vulnerabilities to cause harm, such as malware or cybercriminals. Vulnerabilities are weaknesses or flaws in systems or processes that can be exploited by threats. Exploits are specific techniques or methods used by attackers to take advantage of vulnerabilities and carry out cyber attacks.

1.2. Cybersecurity vs. Information Security

Cybersecurity and information security are often used interchangeably, but they encompass different aspects of protecting digital assets. Cybersecurity is a broad term that refers to the protection of computer systems, networks, and data from cyber threats. It involves a range of practices and technologies designed to defend against attacks that target digital infrastructure. Cybersecurity focuses on safeguarding everything from personal devices and home networks to complex corporate systems and national critical infrastructure. It encompasses various domains, including network security, application security, and operational security.

Information security, on the other hand, is a subset of cybersecurity that specifically focuses on protecting data and information from unauthorized access, use, disclosure, disruption, modification, or destruction. Information security is concerned with ensuring the confidentiality, integrity, and availability of information, regardless of its form. This can include digital data, as well as physical documents and other types of information. Information security measures include encryption, access controls, data classification, and policies for handling sensitive information.

While cybersecurity and information security overlap in many areas, there are distinct differences in their scope and focus. Cybersecurity is broader and encompasses all aspects of protecting digital infrastructure from cyber threats, including network and system security. Information security is more focused on the protection of data itself, regardless of where it resides. This distinction is important because effective cybersecurity requires a comprehensive approach that includes information security practices, but also addresses other aspects such as network security, endpoint security, and user awareness.

The relationship between cybersecurity and information security is complementary. Effective cybersecurity strategies incorporate information security principles to protect data from unauthorized access and ensure its integrity and availability. At the same time, information security relies on cybersecurity measures to safeguard the systems and networks where data is stored and transmitted. Together, they form a holistic approach to protecting digital assets and mitigating the risks associated with cyber threats.

1.3. The Role of Cybersecurity in Modern Society

In modern society, cybersecurity plays a critical role in maintaining trust and confidence in the digital ecosystem. It ensures the confidentiality, integrity, and availability of data, which are essential for the smooth operation of businesses, government functions, and daily life. Effective cybersecurity measures protect against financial losses, reputational damage, and legal repercussions, providing a foundation for innovation and growth in the digital age.

Moreover, cybersecurity is not just a technical issue; it is a societal one. It involves ethical considerations, legal frameworks, and international cooperation. As cyber threats continue to evolve, the need for a collective and coordinated approach to cybersecurity becomes increasingly apparent. This involves not only technical solutions but also education, awareness, and the development of a cybersecurity culture. By understanding its importance, scope, and evolution, and by adopting the best practices outlined in this book, individuals and organizations can contribute to a safer and more secure digital environment.

Here are some of The Role of Cybersecurity in Modern Society:

1. Maintaining Trust and Confidence in the Digital Ecosystem:

Ensuring the security of digital transactions and interactions to build and sustain public trust.

2. Protecting Confidentiality, Integrity, and Availability of Data:

Safeguarding sensitive information from unauthorized access, ensuring data accuracy, and making sure systems are accessible when needed.

3. Preventing Financial Losses, Reputational Damage, and Legal Repercussions:

Implementing measures to avoid the costly impacts of cyber attacks on individuals and organizations.

4. Supporting Innovation and Growth:

Providing a secure foundation that allows businesses and technologies to evolve and expand without the fear of cyber threats.

5. Addressing Ethical, Legal, and Societal Considerations:

Developing and enforcing policies, regulations, and best practices that govern the ethical use of technology and protect against cybercrime.

6. Promoting Education and Awareness:

Raising awareness about cyber threats and educating the public on safe practices to enhance overall cybersecurity posture.

7. Fostering International Cooperation:

Encouraging collaboration among nations to tackle global cyber threats through shared knowledge and coordinated defense strategies.

CHAPTER **2**

TYPES OF CYBER THREATS

Cyber threats encompass a wide range of malicious activities that aim to disrupt, damage, or gain unauthorized access to computer systems, networks, and data. These threats can originate from various sources, including cybercriminals, hackers, nation-states, and insider threats. Common types of cyber threats include malware, phishing and social engineering attacks, Distributed Denial-of-Service (DDoS) attacks, Manin-the-Middle (MitM) attacks, insider threats, and Advanced Persistent Threats (APTs). Each of these threats presents unique challenges and requires specific countermeasures to detect, prevent, and mitigate their impact.

2.1. Malware

Malware, short for malicious software, refers to any software intentionally designed to cause harm to a computer, server, client, or network. It includes a variety of forms, such as viruses, worms, Trojans, and ransomware, each with its own mechanisms and objectives. Malware can be used to steal sensitive information, disrupt operations, or gain unauthorized access to systems. The proliferation of malware poses significant risks to individuals and organizations, requiring robust defenses to detect and neutralize these threats.

Below are part of the types of Malware:

- ✓ **Viruses**: A virus attaches itself to a legitimate program or file and spreads to other programs and files when the host is executed. It requires human intervention to propagate, typically spreading through infected email attachments, software downloads, or compromised websites. Once activated, viruses can corrupt or delete data, disrupt system operations, and create backdoors for other malicious activities.

- ✓ **Worms:** Unlike viruses, worms are standalone malicious programs that replicate themselves to spread to other computers. Worms exploit vulnerabilities in network protocols or software to infect new systems without user intervention. They can cause significant damage by consuming bandwidth, overloading servers, and facilitating the spread of other malware.

- ✓ **Trojans:** A Trojan, or Trojan horse, disguises itself as legitimate software to trick users into installing it. Once installed, Trojans can create backdoors for attackers to access the system, steal data, or install additional malware. Trojans are often used in conjunction with phishing attacks to deceive users into downloading and executing malicious files.

- ✓ **Ransomware:** Ransomware encrypts a victim's data and demands payment, usually in cryptocurrency, to restore access. This type of malware can cause severe disruptions, especially in critical sectors like health care and finance. Ransomware attacks often start with phishing emails that trick users into downloading malicious attachments or clicking on harmful links.

2.2. Phishing and Social Engineering

Phishing and social engineering attacks exploit human psychology to deceive individuals into divulging sensitive information or performing actions that compromise security. These attacks are often carried out through emails, messages, or phone calls that appear to come from legitimate sources. Phishing attacks can lead to significant data breaches, financial losses, and reputational damage, making them a major concern for organizations and individuals alike.

Phishing involves sending fraudulent communications, typically emails, that appear to come from reputable sources, such as banks, government agencies, or trusted companies. The goal is to trick recipients into clicking on malicious links or downloading attachments that install malware or lead to credential theft. Phishing emails often contain urgent messages or threats to create a sense of urgency, compelling recipients to act quickly without verifying the authenticity of the message.

Types of Phishing:

✓ **Spear Phishing:** A targeted form of phishing aimed at specific individuals or organizations. Spear phishing emails are often personalized, making them more convincing and increasing the likelihood of success. Attackers may gather information about their targets from social media or other sources to craft more believable messages.

✓ **Whaling:** A sub type of spear phishing that targets high-profile individuals, such as executives or senior officials, within an organization. Whaling attacks often focus on business-related topics and use sophisticated tactics to bypass security measures and exploit the trust placed in these individuals.

✓ **Clone Phishing:** Involves duplicating a legitimate email previously sent by the target, replacing any legitimate links or attachments with malicious ones. The attacker resends the email, often claiming it is a follow-up or an updated version, making it more likely for the recipient to trust and interact with the malicious content.

Social engineering goes beyond phishing by exploiting various psychological manipulation techniques to trick individuals into revealing confidential information or performing actions that compromise security. Social engineering attacks can take many forms, including:

✓ **Pretexting:** The attacker creates a fabricated scenario (pretext) to obtain sensitive information from the target. This could involve posing as a trusted authority figure or service provider to gain the victim's trust and extract information such as passwords, credit card numbers, or personal details.

✓ **Baiting:** The attacker entices the victim with the promise of a reward or benefit, such as free software, movie downloads, or USB drives left in public places. When the victim takes the bait and interacts with the malicious content, their system becomes compromised.

✓ **Tailgating:** Also known as piggybacking, tailgating involves gaining unauthorized physical access to a restricted area by following someone with authorized access. The attacker may rely on the victim's courtesy or distraction to gain entry without raising suspicion.

Organizations can mitigate the risks of phishing and social engineering by implementing comprehensive security awareness programs that educate employees about recognizing and responding to these threats. Technical measures, such as email filters, multi-factor authentication, and anti-phishing tools, can also help detect and block phishing attempts. Regular security assessments and simulated phishing exercises can further enhance an organization's resilience against these types of attacks.

2.3. DDoS Attacks

Distributed Denial-of-Service (DDoS) attacks aim to overwhelm a target's network, server, or application with a flood of traffic, rendering it unavailable to legitimate users. These attacks leverage multiple compromised devices, often part of a botnet, to generate massive volumes of traffic and exhaust the target's resources. DDoS attacks can cause significant disruptions, financial losses, and reputational damage, making them a critical concern for businesses and service providers.

DDoS attacks can be classified into several types based on their methods and targets:

- ✓ **Volume-Based Attacks:** These attacks focus on saturating the bandwidth of the target with high volumes of traffic, overwhelming the network infrastructure. Examples include UDP floods, ICMP floods, and amplification attacks. Volume-based attacks aim to consume all available bandwidth, preventing legitimate traffic from reaching the target.

- ✓ **Protocol Attacks:** These attacks exploit weaknesses in network protocols to consume server resources and disrupt service. Examples include SYN floods, Ping of Death, and Smurf attacks. Protocol attacks often target specific protocol vulnerabilities to exhaust the processing capacity of the target's systems.

- ✓ **Application Layer Attacks:** These attacks target specific applications or services with the intent of exhausting their resources and causing service disruption. Examples include

HTTP floods, Slowloris attacks, and DNS query floods. Application layer attacks are often more sophisticated and harder to detect because they generate legitimate-looking traffic that mimics normal user behavior.

The impact of DDoS attacks can be devastating, especially for online businesses, financial institutions, and critical infrastructure. Prolonged downtime can lead to significant revenue losses, erode customer trust, and damage the organization's reputation. In some cases, DDoS attacks are used as a smokescreen to divert attention from other malicious activities, such as data breaches or malware infections.

To defend against DDoS attacks, organizations can implement various mitigation strategies:

- ✓ **Network and Application Layer Protection:** Deploying DDoS protection services and appliances that can detect and mitigate attacks in real-time. These solutions often use traffic analysis and filtering techniques to identify and block malicious traffic while allowing legitimate traffic to pass through.

- ✓ **Content Delivery Networks (CDNs):** Using CDNs to distribute traffic across multiple servers and locations, reducing the impact of DDoS attacks on any single point. CDNs can absorb and disperse traffic surges, helping maintain service availability during an attack.

- ✓ **Rate Limiting and Throttling:** Implementing rate limiting and throttling mechanisms to control the volume of traffic that can reach the target's systems. This can help prevent overload and maintain service availability for legitimate users.

- ✓ **Redundancy and Load Balancing:** Designing networks and systems with redundancy and load balancing to distribute traffic across multiple servers and data centers. This can help ensure that no single point of failure becomes overwhelmed during an attack.

2.4. Man-in-the-Middle Attacks

Man-in-the-Middle (MitM) attacks involve an attacker intercepting and potentially altering communications between two parties without their knowledge. This type of attack can compromise the confidentiality and integrity of data exchanged, allowing the attacker to eavesdrop on conversations, steal sensitive information, or manipulate the content of the communication. MitM attacks pose significant risks to online transactions, communications, and data transfers, making them a critical concern for cybersecurity.

MitM attacks can be executed through various methods:

- ✓ **Eavesdropping:** The attacker intercepts and monitors the communication between two parties without altering the data. This allows the attacker to gather sensitive information, such as login credentials, credit card numbers, and personal details. Eavesdropping can be conducted using tools like packet sniffers or by exploiting vulnerabilities in network protocols.

- ✓ **Session Hijacking:** The attacker takes over an active session between a user and a service by stealing the session token or cookie. This allows the attacker to impersonate the user and gain unauthorized access to the service. Session hijacking can be performed through methods like cross-site scripting (XSS) or network-level attacks.

- ✓ **SSL Stripping:** The attacker downgrades the secure HTTPS connection to an unencrypted HTTP connection, allowing them to intercept and manipulate the data transmitted. SSL stripping exploits vulnerabilities in the implementation of SSL/TLS protocols to deceive users into believing they are communicating over a secure channel.

✓ **DNS Spoofing:** The attacker manipulates the Domain NameSystem (DNS) responses to redirect users to malicious websites. DNS spoofing can be used to intercept and alter communications, steal sensitive information, or distribute malware. MitM attacks can be mitigated through various security measures:

✓ **Encryption:** Using strong encryption protocols, such as SSL/TLS, to secure communications and protect data from interception and tampering. Encryption ensures that even if the data is intercepted, it cannot be easily read or modified by the attacker.

✓ **Authentication:** Implementing robust authentication mechanisms, such as multi-factor authentication (MFA), to verify the identities of communicating parties. Authentication helps prevent unauthorized access and session hijacking.

✓ **Network Security:** Securing network infrastructure with firewalls, intrusion detection systems (IDS), and intrusion prevention systems (IPS) to detect and block MitM attacks. Network security measures can help identify and mitigate suspicious activities that may indicate an ongoing attack.

✓ **DNS Security:** Implementing DNS security extensions (DNSSEC) to protect DNS responses from spoofing and ensure the integrity of DNS records. DNSSEC helps prevent attackers from redirecting users to malicious websites.

2.5. Insider Threats

Insider threats involve individuals within an organization who misuse their access to compromise security, steal data, or cause harm to the organization. These threats can come from employees, contractors, or business partners with authorized access to sensitive information and systems. Insider threats can be challenging to detect and mitigate because they involve trusted individuals with legitimate access rights.

Insider threats can be classified into several categories:

✓ **Malicious Insiders:** Individuals who intentionally misuse their access for personal gain, financial profit, or to cause harm to the organization. Malicious insiders may steal sensitive data, sabotage systems, or sell confidential information to competitors or cybercriminals.

✓ **Negligent Insiders:** Individuals who unintentionally compromise security through careless actions or lack of awareness. Negligent insiders may fall victim to phishing attacks, inadvertently disclose sensitive information, or fail to follow security policies and procedures.

Compromised Insiders: Individuals whose accounts orcredentials have been compromised by external attackers. Compromised insiders may unknowingly facilitate unauthorized access and malicious activities by cybercriminals using their credentials.

Mitigating insider threats requires a combination of technical, organizational, and human measures:

✓ **Access Controls:** Implementing strict access controls and the principle of least privilege to limit access to sensitive information and systems. Access should be granted based on the individual's role and responsibilities, and regularly reviewed to ensure appropriateness.

✓ **Monitoring and Auditing:** Deploying monitoring and auditing tools to detect unusual or suspicious activities by insiders. Continuous monitoring can help identify potential insider threats and take timely action to mitigate risks.

✓ **User Education and Awareness:** Conducting regular security awareness training to educate employees about the risks of insider threats and the importance of following security policies. Training should cover safe practices, recognizing phishing attempts, and reporting suspicious activities.

✓ **Behavioral Analysis:** Using behavioral analysis and anomaly detection techniques to identify deviations from normal user behavior. Behavioral analysis can help detect potential insider threats based on patterns of access, data usage, and other indicators.

2.6. Advanced Persistent Threats (APTs)

Advanced Persistent Threats (APTs) are sophisticated, targeted cyber attacks carried out by well-funded and organized threat actors, often with political or economic motivations. APTs aim to gain long-term access to a target's network to steal sensitive information, disrupt operations, or conduct espionage. These attacks are characterized by their persistence, stealth, and ability to evade traditional security measures, making them a significant threat to national security, critical infrastructure, and large organizations.

APTs typically follow a multi-stage attack lifecycle:

✓ **Initial Compromise:** The attacker gains a foothold in the target's network through methods such as phishing, exploiting vulnerabilities, or using zero-day exploits. The initial compromise often involves installing malware or backdoors to maintain access.

✓ **Establishing Persistence:** Once inside the network, the attacker deploys additional tools and techniques to ensure long-term access. This may involve creating hidden accounts, installing rootkits, or using remote access tools (RATs) to maintain control over compromised systems.

✓ **Privilege Escalation:** The attacker seeks to escalate privileges to gain higher levels of access within the target's network. This may involve exploiting vulnerabilities, stealing credentials, or leveraging misconfigurations to gain administrative rights.

✓ **Lateral Movement:** The attacker moves laterally within the network to identify and access valuable assets. Lateral movement techniques include using compromised credentials, exploiting trust relationships, and leveraging legitimate administrative tools.

✓ **Data Exfiltration:** The attacker identifies and extracts valuable data from the target's network. Data exfiltration methods may include compressing and encrypting data, using covert channels, or disguising exfiltration traffic as legitimate communications.

✓ **Covering Tracks:** The attacker takes steps to evade detection and maintain access, such as deleting logs, using encryption, and employing anti-forensic techniques. Covering tracks helps the attacker remain undetected and continue their activities over an extended period.

Defending against APTs requires a comprehensive and muti-layered approach:

✓ **Threat Intelligence:** Leveraging threat intelligence to stay informed about the latest APT tactics, techniques, and procedures (TTPs). Threat intelligence helps organizations proactively identify and respond to emerging threats.

✓ **Network Segmentation:** Implementing network segmentation to limit the attacker's ability to move laterally within the network. Network segmentation can contain the impact of an APT and protect critical assets.

✓ **Endpoint Detection and Response (EDR):** Deploying EDR solutions to monitor and analyze endpoint activities for signs of compromise. EDR tools can detect and respond to suspicious behaviors and anomalies indicative of APT activities.

✓ **Incident Response Planning:** Developing and regularly testing incident response plans to ensure a swift and effective response to APT incidents. Incident response plans should include procedures for detecting, containing, and eradicating threats, as well as communication and recovery strategies.

✓ **User Education and Awareness:** Training employees to recognize and report potential APT activities, such as phishing attempts and unusual system behaviors. Educating users about the risks of APTs and safe practices can enhance the organization's overall security posture.

Understanding the various types of cyber threats, from malware and phishing to advanced persistent threats, is crucial for developing effective cybersecurity strategies. Each type of threat presents unique challenges and requires specific countermeasures to protect against potential attacks. By implementing a combination of technical, organizational, and human-focused measures, organizations can enhance their resilience against cyber threats and safeguard their digital assets in an increasingly complex threat landscape.

CHAPTER

3

CYBER ATTACK VECTORS

C yber attack vectors are the methods or pathways used by cyber attackers to infiltrate computer systems, networks, or devices. These vectors exploit vulnerabilities in software, hardware, and human behavior to deliver malicious payloads or gain unauthorized access. Understanding these vectors is crucial for developing effective defensive strategies and protecting against potential threats. Common cyber attack vectors include network-based attacks, application-based attacks, physical attacks, and social engineering tactics.

Network-based attacks exploit weaknesses in network infrastructure to intercept, manipulate, or disrupt communications between devices. These attacks can target various layers of the network, from physical hardware to application protocols. Examples include Distributed Denialof-Service (DDoS) attacks, which overwhelm a network with traffic, and Man-in-the-Middle (MitM) attacks, which intercept and alter communications between two parties. Network security measures such as firewalls, intrusion detection systems, and encryption are essential to defend against these types of attacks.

Application-based attacks target software applications by exploiting vulnerabilities in their code or design. These attacks can result in unauthorized access, data breaches, or system disruptions. Common application-based attack vectors include SQL injection, which manipulates database queries to execute malicious code, and Cross-Site Scripting (XSS), which injects malicious scripts into web pages viewed by other users. Regular code reviews, vulnerability assessments, and the use of secure coding practices are vital for mitigating the risks associated with application-based attacks.

3.1. Network-Based Attacks

Network-based attacks target the infrastructure and communication channels of computer networks to compromise data integrity, confidentiality, or availability. These attacks exploit vulnerabilities within network protocols, services, or configurations, aiming to disrupt normal network operations or gain unauthorized access to sensitive information. Given the central role networks play in modern organizations, securing them against such attacks is vital to maintaining overall cybersecurity.

One common type of network-based attack is the Distributed Denial of Service (DDoS attack, where attackers use multiple compromised systems to flood a target network with excessive traffic, overwhelming its resources and causing service outages. Another prevalent attack is Man-in-the-Middle (MitM), where attackers intercept and potentially alter communications between two parties without their knowledge. This can lead to eavesdropping on sensitive information or injecting malicious data into the communication stream. Additionally, Network Sniffing involves capturing and analyzing network traffic to extract confidential data, such as login credentials or proprietary information.

Port scanning is another technique used by attackers to identify open and vulnerable ports on networked systems, which can be exploited for further attacks. Exploiting network services involves taking advantage of known vulnerabilities in network services or protocols to gain unauthorized access or control over systems. Spoofing attacks, such as IP spoofing or DNS spoofing, trick systems into believing they are communicating with a trusted source, potentially leading to unauthorized access or redirection of traffic. Protecting against these network-based threats requires a combination of robust firewall rules, intrusion detection systems, encryption, and regular network monitoring to ensure the integrity and security of network communications.

✓ **Eavesdropping:** Eavesdropping, or sniffing, involves intercepting and monitoring network communications to gather sensitive information such as username, passwords, or credit card numbers. Attackers use tools like packet sniffers to capture data packets as they travel across the network. Eavesdropping can occur on both wired and wireless networks, with wireless networks being particularly vulnerable due to the broadcast nature of wireless signals. Encrypting communications using protocols like SSL/TLS and implementing strong network security measures can help protect against eavesdropping.

✓ **Spoofing:** Spoofing attacks involve an attacker impersonating a legitimate device or user to gain unauthorized access to systems or data. This can include IP spoofing, where an attacker sends packets with a forged source IP address, or email spoofing, where an attacker sends emails that appear to come from a trusted source. Spoofing can lead to various malicious activities, including data theft, phishing, and Man-in-the-Middle attacks. Implementing authentication mechanisms, such as digital certificates and two-factor authentication, can help mitigate spoofing risks.

3.2. Application Based Attacks

Application-based attacks target software applications, exploiting vulnerabilities within them to compromise systems or data. These attacks are often executed through methods that exploit weaknesses in the application's code, its configuration, or its interactions with other systems. Attackers may leverage these vulnerabilities to gain unauthorized access, execute malicious code, or steal sensitive information. As applications become increasingly complex and interconnected, the potential attack surface grows, making them a prime target for cybercriminals.

Common types of application-based attacks include:

✓ **SQL Injection:** SQL Injection attacks exploit vulnerabilities in web applications that interact with databases. By inserting malicious SQL code into input fields, attackers can manipulate database queries to execute unauthorized commands. This can lead to data breaches, data loss, or unauthorized administrative access to the database. To prevent SQL Injection, developers should use prepared statements and parameterized queries, which separate SQL code from user input, and perform thorough input validation and sanitization.

✓ **Cross-Site Scripting (XSS):** Cross-Site Scripting (XSS) attacks occur when an attacker injects malicious scripts into web pages viewed by other users. These scripts can execute in the victim's browser, potentially stealing session cookies, redirecting users to malicious websites, or performing actions on behalf of the user. XSS can be classified into three types: stored XSS, where the malicious script is permanently stored on the target server; reflected XSS, where the script is reflected off a web server; and DOM-based XSS, where the vulnerability exists in the client-side code. Preventing XSS involves validating and sanitizing all user inputs, encoding output data, and implementing content security policies.

In addition to these, **remote code execution (RCE)** attacks allow attackers to run arbitrary code on a victim's machine by exploiting vulnerabilities in the application. **Buffer overflow attacks** occur when more data is written to a buffer than it can handle, potentially overwriting adjacent memory and allowing execution of malicious code. **File inclusion attacks**, such as Local File Inclusion (LFI) or Remote File Inclusion (RFI), enable attackers to include files from a local or remote server, which can lead to unauthorized data access or code execution. Each of these attack vectors underscores the need for robust application security practices, including regular updates, code reviews, and secure coding standards.

3.3. Physical Attacks

Physical attacks involve direct, tangible actions to compromise the security of systems, devices, or facilities. Unlike digital attacks, physical attacks target hardware or infrastructure, often requiring the attacker to be in close proximity to the target. These attacks can bypass traditional cybersecurity defenses by exploiting physical access to sensitive equipment or locations. Effective physical security measures are crucial to prevent unauthorized individuals from gaining access and causing harm.

Examples of physical attacks include **theft or tampering** with hardware. For instance, stealing laptops, servers, or other devices can lead to data breaches if these devices contain sensitive information. Direct access attacks involve physically accessing secure areas, such as data centers, to manipulate or damage equipment. Attackers might use techniques like social engineering to gain access to restricted areas, posing as legitimate personnel to exploit security weaknesses.

Physical sabotage is another form of attack where attackers intentionally damage or destroy hardware to disrupt operations. For example, they might tamper with server components or disable critical infrastructure to cause downtime or operational failure. Insider threats can also involve physical attacks, where employees or contractors with authorized access misuse their privileges to cause harm. Such attacks highlight the importance of robust physical security protocols, including surveillance, access controls, and employee training to mitigate risks and protect assets from physical threats.

✓ **Unauthorized Access:** Unauthorized access involves gaining physical entry to secure areas or systems without permission. This can include accessing server rooms, data centers, or individual devices to steal data, install malicious software, or tamper with hardware. Physical access controls, such as biometric authentication, key card access, and surveillance systems, are essential for preventing unauthorized access. Regular security audits and employee training can also help identify and mitigate potential physical security risks.

✓ **Hardware Tampering:** Hardware tampering involves altering physical components of a device to compromise its security or functionality. This can include installing hardware keyloggers, modifying circuit boards, or replacing genuine components with malicious ones. Hardware tampering can lead to data breaches, system failures, or the introduction of backdoors for remote access. Protecting against hardware tampering requires robust physical security measures, regular inspections of hardware, and the use of tamper-evident seals and enclosures. Implementing supply chain security practices can also help ensure the integrity of hardware components throughout their lifecycle.

CHAPTER 4

THREAT DETECTION

Threat detection is a critical aspect of cybersecurity that involves identifying and responding to potential security threats before they can cause significant harm. This process requires a combination of advanced technologies, methodologies, and human expertise to effectively monitor, analyze, and respond to suspicious activities. Effective threat detection can prevent data breaches, minimize the impact of attacks, and protect the integrity, confidentiality, and availability of information systems.

In an increasingly complex cyber threat landscape, organizations must implement robust threat detection mechanisms to safeguard their digital assets. This includes deploying various detection techniques, such as signature-based detection, anomaly-based detection, behavioral analysis, and leveraging threat intelligence. By integrating these approaches, organizations can improve their ability to detect and respond to both known and unknown threats, enhancing their overall security posture.

4.1. Overview of Threat Detection

Threat detection involves continuous monitoring and analysis of network traffic, system logs, and user behavior to identify potential security incidents. This proactive approach helps organizations recognize and respond to threats in real-time, mitigating the risk of data breaches and minimizing the impact of cyber attacks. Effective threat detection relies on a combination of automated tools, advanced analytics, and human expertise to accurately identify and respond to threats.

The importance of early detection cannot be overstated. Early detection allows organizations to respond to threats before they can cause significant damage, reducing the potential for data loss, financial harm, and reputational damage. By identifying threats at an early stage, organizations can implement appropriate countermeasures, such as isolating affected systems, patching vulnerabilities, and strengthening security controls to prevent future incidents.

Importance of Early Detection

1. **Minimizes Damage and Disruption:** Early detection allows organizations to identify and respond to potential threats before they can cause significant damage or disruption. By catching security incidents in their early stages, organizations can prevent data breaches, system outages, and other adverse effects that could impact business operations. This proactive approach helps to limit the extent of the damage and reduces the overall impact on the organization.

2. **Reduces Recovery Time and Costs:** Detecting threats early can significantly reduce the time and costs associated with recovery. Early intervention allows organizations to implement remediation measures quickly, mitigating the need for extensive recovery efforts.

This reduces downtime, minimizes financial losses, and lowers the costs associated with incident response, forensic investigations, and system repairs.

3. **Protects Sensitive Data:** Early detection helps safeguard sensitive and confidential data from being compromised or stolen. By identifying potential threats before they can access or exfiltrate sensitive information, organizations can protect their data assets and maintain the confidentiality and integrity of their information. This is crucial for maintaining customer trust and compliance with data protection regulations.

4. **Maintains Business Continuity:** Identifying and addressing threats at an early stage ensures that business operations can continue with minimal disruption. By preventing or quickly resolving security incidents, organizations can maintain normal operations and avoid interruptions that could impact productivity and service delivery. This is essential for maintaining business continuity and ensuring that operations run smoothly.

5. **Enhances Overall Security Posture:** Early detection contributes to an organization's overall security posture by improving its ability to respond to threats effectively. By continuously monitoring for and addressing potential threats, organizations can strengthen their security measures, adapt to emerging threats, and reduce vulnerabilities. This proactive approach enhances the organization's resilience against future attacks and improves its overall security strategy.

Detection Techniques and Tools

✓ Signature-Based Detection

✓ Anomaly-Based Detection

✓ Behavioral Analysis

✓ Threat Intelligence Platforms

✓ Intrusion Detection Systems (IDS)

✓ Security Information and Event Management (SIEM) Systems

4.2. Signature-Based Detection

Signature-based detection involves identifying threats by comparing observed behaviors or patterns against a database of known threat signatures. These signatures are unique identifiers, such as specific strings of code or known malware patterns, that match previously identified threats. This method is highly effective at detecting known threats and is commonly used in antivirus software and intrusion detection systems (IDS).

While signature-based detection is efficient and reliable for identifying known threats, it has limitations. It cannot detect new, unknown threats or variants of existing threats that do not match any known signature. This makes it less effective against zero-day attacks and sophisticated malware that constantly evolves to evade detection. Despite these limitations, signature-based detection remains a crucial component of a muti-layered security strategy, providing a strong defense against wellknown and documented threats.

Organizations can enhance the effectiveness of signature-based detection by regularly updating their threat signature databases. This ensures that the detection systems are equipped with the latest information on emerging threats, improving their ability to identify and block known malicious activities. Combining signature-based detection with other detection techniques can provide comprehensive protection against a wide range of cyber threats.

4.3. Anomaly-Based Detection

Anomaly-based detection involves identifying deviations from normal behavior or established baselines within a system or network. By monitoring and analyzing typical patterns of activity, such as network traffic, user behavior, or system performance, anomaly-based detection can flag unusual activities that may indicate a potential threat. This method is particularly effective at detecting new or unknown threats that do not have predefined signatures.

One of the main advantages of anomaly-based detection is its ability to identify zero-day attacks and sophisticated threats that traditional signature-based methods might miss. However, this approach can also generate false positives, as legitimate activities that deviate from established baselines may be mistakenly flagged as threats. To mitigate this, anomaly-based detection systems often incorporate machine learning algorithms to improve accuracy and reduce the occurrence of false alarms over time.

Implementing anomaly-based detection requires a thorough understanding of normal system behavior and continuous monitoring to maintain up-to-date baselines. By integrating this method with other detection techniques, organizations can achieve a more comprehensive security posture, capable of identifying both known and unknown threats in real-time. Anomaly-based detection is a crucial component of modern threat detection strategies, providing a proactive approach to identifying and responding to emerging cyber threats.

4.4. Behavioral Analysis

Behavioral analysis involves monitoring and analyzing the behavior of users, systems, and applications to identify potential security threats. This method focuses on understanding the typical patterns of activity and detecting deviations that may indicate malicious intent. Behavioral analysis can uncover insider threats, advanced persistent threats

(APTs), and other sophisticated attacks that might bypass traditional detection methods.

One of the key benefits of behavioral analysis is its ability to detect threats based on the context of activities rather than relying solely on predefined signatures or anomalies. By understanding the normal behavior of users and systems, security teams can identify subtle indicators of compromise, such as unusual login times, atypical data access patterns, or unexpected changes in system configurations. This contextual awareness helps organizations detect and respond to threats more effectively.

Implementing behavioral analysis requires advanced analytics and machine learning techniques to continuously learn and adapt to evolving behaviors. Security Information and Event Management (SIEM) systems and User and Entity Behavior Analytics (UEBA) platforms often incorporate behavioral analysis to provide comprehensive threat detection capabilities. By combining behavioral analysis with other detection methods, organizations can enhance their ability to identify and mitigate a wide range of security threats.

4.5. Threat Intelligence

Threat intelligence involves the collection, analysis, and dissemination of information about current and emerging threats. This information, gathered from various sources such as threat feeds, security researchers, and industry reports, provides insights into the tactics, techniques, and procedures (TTPs) used by cyber attackers. By leveraging threat intelligence, organizations can stay informed about the latest threats and proactively strengthen their defenses.

One of the primary benefits of threat intelligence is its ability to provide context and actionable information that can be used to enhance threat detection and response efforts. For example, threat intelligence can help security teams identify indicators of compromise (IOCs), such as specific IP addresses, domain names, or file hashes associated with known threats. By integrating this information into their detection systems, organizations can improve their ability to identify and block malicious activities.

Effective threat intelligence requires collaboration and information sharing among organizations, industry groups, and government agencies. By participating in threat intelligence sharing initiatives, organizations can gain access to a broader range of information and insights, improving their overall security posture. Implementing threat intelligence platforms and integrating them with existing security tools, such as SIEM systems, can further enhance an organization's ability to detect and respond to threats in real-time.

CHAPTER 5

PREVENTION TECHNIQUES

Prevention techniques are essential in cybersecurity for mitigating risks and protecting systems before threats can exploit vulnerabilities. These techniques involve proactive measures to defend against various types of cyber threats, such as malware, unauthorized access, and network intrusions. By implementing a layered security approach that includes multiple prevention strategies, organizations can significantly reduce the likelihood of successful attacks and enhance their overall security posture.

One fundamental aspect of prevention is maintaining up-to-date security technologies and protocols. This includes regularly updating software and systems to patch vulnerabilities, employing strong authentication mechanisms, and configuring security devices to detect and block malicious activities. Prevention also involves educating users about safe practices and potential threats, ensuring they recognize and respond appropriately to suspicious activities such as phishing emails and social engineering tactics.

Additionally, effective prevention requires continuous monitoring and analysis to identify potential weaknesses and address them promptly. This involves using security tools and technologies, conducting regular security assessments, and applying best practices in system configuration and network management. By integrating these approaches into a cohesive security strategy, organizations can proactively defend against cyber threats and maintain the integrity and availability of their information systems.

5.1. Basic Preventive Measures

✓ **Firewalls:** Firewalls serve as a critical line of defense by controlling the flow of traffic between networks. They can be hardware or software-based and are designed to block or allow traffic based on predefined security rules. Firewalls help prevent unauthorized access to internal networks and systems, and they can be configured to filter out malicious traffic and protect against various types of attacks.

✓ **Antivirus Software:** Antivirus software is designed to detect, quarantine, and remove malicious software such as viruses, worms, and Trojans. It works by scanning files and programs for known malware signatures and monitoring system behavior for suspicious activities. Regular updates to antivirus software are crucial for ensuring that it can recognize and protect against the latest threats.

✓ **Anti-Malware Tools:** Anti-malware tools go beyond traditional antivirus software by providing more comprehensive protection against various types of malware, including ransomware and spyware. These tools often include advanced features such as realtime scanning, behavioral analysis, and automatic updates to defend against evolving threats. They help detect and remove malware that might not be identified by traditional antivirus solutions.

5.2. Network Security

Intrusion Prevention Systems (IPS) build on the capabilities of IDS by not only detecting but also actively preventing threats in real-time. IPS systems analyze network traffic to identify and block malicious activities automatically, stopping potential attacks before they can reach critical systems or data. They work by enforcing security policies and applying defensive measures, such as blocking malicious IP addresses or disrupting harmful traffic patterns. By integrating IPS with existing security infrastructure, organizations can enhance their ability to respond to threats swiftly and maintain a robust security posture. Intrusion Detection Systems (IDS): IDS monitor network traffic for signs of suspicious or unauthorized activities. They analyze data packets and network flows to detect potential threats or attacks. IDS can generate alerts when anomalies or known attack patterns are identified, allowing security teams to investigate and respond to potential intrusions.

5.3. Endpoint Security

Endpoint security refers to the strategies and technologies used to protect individual devices connected to a network, such as computers, smartphones, tablets, and other endpoints. These devices are often entry points for cyber threats, making their security crucial for safeguarding an organization's overall IT infrastructure. Endpoint security involves implementing measures to prevent, detect, and respond to threats that may compromise these devices, ensuring that each endpoint remains a secure and integral part of the network.

A fundamental component of endpoint security is the use of antivirus and anti-malware software, which scans devices for known threats and prevents malicious software from executing. Additionally, firewalls on individual devices can block unauthorized access attempts and filter incoming and outgoing traffic. Endpoint Detection and Response

(EDR) solutions provide advanced monitoring and analysis capabilities, allowing for the detection of suspicious behavior and rapid response to potential threats. Regular patch management and software updates are also crucial, as they address known vulnerabilities and enhance the security posture of the devices.

✓ Access controls and authentication mechanisms further bolster endpoint security by ensuring that only authorized users can access specific devices and data. This includes implementing strong password policies, multi-factor authentication (MFA), and role-based access controls. Encryption of data stored on endpoints protects sensitive information from being exposed if a device is lost or stolen. Overall, a comprehensive endpoint security strategy involves combining these technologies and practices to create a multi-layered defense, minimizing the risk of breaches and ensuring the integrity of the network as a whole.

✓ **Securing Devices:** Securing devices involves implementing measures to protect individual computers, servers, and other endpoints from threats. This includes applying security patches, configuring device settings to enhance security, and using endpoint protection software to detect and prevent malware infections. Properly securing devices helps prevent them from becoming entry points for attackers.

✓ **Mobile Device Management (MDM):** MDM refers to the administration and security of mobile devices such as smartphones and tablets. It involves deploying policies and tools to manage and secure mobile devices, including enforcing encryption, controlling app installations, and remotely wiping devices in case of loss or theft. MDM helps ensure that mobile devices are protected against threats and comply with organizational security policies.

5.4. Email and Web Security

Email and web security are critical components of overall cybersecurity, focusing on protecting communication and browsing activities from various threats. Emails and web interactions are common vectors for cyberattacks, such as phishing, malware distribution, and data breaches.

Ensuring the security of these channels is essential to safeguarding sensitive information and maintaining the integrity of communications. Email security involves implementing measures to protect against threats that can compromise email accounts or the content of emails. This includes spam filters to block unwanted or potentially malicious messages, and anti-phishing tools to detect and prevent deceptive emails that attempt to trick users into disclosing personal information. Email encryption ensures that sensitive communications are protected from unauthorized access during transmission. Additionally, multi-factor authentication (MFA) adds an extra layer of security by requiring multiple forms of verification before granting access to email accounts. Web security focuses on protecting users while they browse the internet, including safeguarding against threats like malicious websites and attacks on web applications. Secure browsing practices, such as using HTTPS to encrypt data transmitted between a user and a website, are crucial. Web filters can block access to harmful sites known for distributing malware or phishing scams. Regular updates and patches to web browsers and plugins help address known vulnerabilities that could be exploited by attackers. By integrating these security measures, organizations and individuals can significantly reduce the risk of encountering threats while using email and the web.

✓ **Secure Email Gateways:** Secure email gateways protect against email-based threats by filtering and blocking malicious content such as phishing emails, spam, and malware attachments. They analyze incoming and outgoing email traffic to identify and prevent potential threats, ensuring that only legitimate and safe emails reach their intended recipients.

✓ **Web Application Firewalls (WAF):** WAFs protect web applications from various types of attacks, including SQL injection, cross-site scripting (XSS), and other web-based threats. They monitor and filter HTTP traffic to detect and block malicious requests before they reach the web application. WAFs help safeguard web applications by providing an additional layer of security beyond traditional network firewalls.

CHAPTER

6

SECURITY FRAMEWORKS AND STANDARD

Security frameworks and standards provide structured guidelines and best practices for managing and improving cybersecurity practices. These frameworks are designed to help organizations establish, implement, and maintain effective security programs by providing a clear set of principles and requirements. By adhering to these frameworks, organizations can better protect their information assets, ensure compliance with regulations, and reduce the risk of cyber threats. A well-defined security framework typically includes a set of policies, procedures, and controls tailored to address specific security needs. These frameworks help organizations assess their current security posture, identify vulnerabilities, and develop strategies to mitigate risks. They also offer a standardized approach to security management, making it easier to evaluate and improve security practices across different environments and industries.

Security standards complement frameworks by providing specific technical and procedural requirements. Standards serve as benchmarks for measuring the effectiveness of security controls and ensuring consistency in the implementation of security measures. They are often developed by industry groups or international organizations and can be used to demonstrate compliance with regulatory requirements and industry best practices.

Implementing security frameworks and standards helps organizations achieve a higher level of security maturity. It allows them to systematically address security challenges, adopt best practices, and continuously improve their security posture. Furthermore, these frameworks facilitate communication and collaboration between different stakeholders, including management, IT teams, and auditors, by providing a common language and structure for discussing security issues.

By providing structured guidelines and measurable benchmarks, they enable organizations to protect their assets, comply with regulations, and reduce the likelihood of security incidents. Adopting these frameworks ensures that security practices are aligned with industry standards and continuously improved to address evolving threats.

6.1. Overview of Security Frameworks

Security frameworks provide a structured approach to managing and improving cybersecurity. They offer a comprehensive set of guidelines and best practices that organizations can follow to protect their information systems and data. These frameworks help organizations establish a security management program, assess risks, implement controls, and continuously monitor and improve their security posture.

By following a recognized framework, organizations can ensure that their security practices are effective and aligned with industry standards. One of the key benefits of security frameworks is their ability to provide a common language and structure for discussing security issues. This makes it easier for organizations to communicate their security needs, collaborate with stakeholders, and demonstrate compliance with regulations. Security frameworks also offer a systematic approach to identifying and addressing vulnerabilities, allowing organizations to prioritize their security efforts and allocate resources more effectively. Another important aspect of security frameworks is their focus on continuous improvement. Most frameworks emphasize the need for ongoing assessment and refinement of security practices to adapt to evolving threats and technological changes. By regularly reviewing and updating their security measures, organizations can stay ahead of potential risks and ensure that their security programs remain effective and resilient.

Importance and Benefits

Security frameworks and standards are crucial for managing cybersecurity risks effectively. They provide organizations with a structured approach to identifying, assessing, and mitigating security threats. By following established frameworks and standards, organizations can systematically address vulnerabilities, implement appropriate controls, and ensure that their security practices are aligned with industry best practices. This structured approach helps organizations protect their information assets, reduce the likelihood of security incidents, and maintain a robust security posture.

Adhering to security frameworks and standards also facilitates compliance with regulatory requirements. Many industries are subject to specific regulations and standards related to cybersecurity, such as data protection laws and industry-specific guidelines. By implementing recognized frameworks and standards, organizations can demonstrate their commitment to meeting these regulatory requirements and avoid potential penalties or legal issues. Compliance with security standards also enhances an organization's reputation and builds trust with customers, partners, and stakeholders.

In addition to regulatory compliance, security frameworks and standards offer numerous benefits, including improved risk management and resource allocation. Frameworks provide a systematic approach to assessing and managing security risks, allowing organizations to prioritize their security efforts based on potential impact and likelihood. This helps organizations allocate resources more effectively and invest in security measures that address their most critical risks. Furthermore, frameworks often include best practices and recommendations for improving security posture, enabling organizations to stay ahead of emerging threats and maintain a proactive security stance.

Another significant benefit of adopting security frameworks and standards is the ability to benchmark and measure security performance. Frameworks provide a set of criteria and metrics for evaluating the effectiveness of security controls and practices. This allows organizations to track their progress over time, identify areas for improvement, and demonstrate the effectiveness of their security programs to stakeholders. Regular assessment and bench marking help organizations continuously enhance their security posture and ensure that their security measures remain effective in the face of evolving threats.

Finally, security frameworks and standards promote a culture of security within organizations. By establishing clear guidelines and expectations for security practices, frameworks help create a shared understanding of security goals and responsibilities among employees. This fosters a culture of security awareness and encourages individuals at all levels of the organization to prioritize and adhere to security best practices. A strong security culture is essential for maintaining a resilient security posture and ensuring that security measures are consistently implemented and enforced.

6.2. Popular Frameworks

✓ **NIST Cybersecurity Framework:** Developed by the National Institute of Standards and Technology (NIST), this framework provides a comprehensive approach to managing cybersecurity risks. It consists of five core functions: Identify, Protect, Detect, Respond, and Recover. These functions offer a structured approach to understanding and managing cybersecurity risks, from identifying assets and vulnerabilities to responding to incidents and recovering from attacks. The NIST Cybersecurity Framework is widely recognized for its flexibility and applicability across various industries, helping organizations of all sizes improve their cybersecurity posture and resilience.

✓ **ISO/IEC 27001:** The ISO/IEC 27001 standard is an international benchmark for establishing, implementing, maintaining, and continuously improving an information security management system (ISMS). It provides a systematic approach to managing sensitive information and ensuring its confidentiality, integrity, and availability. The standard outlines a set of requirements and controls for risk assessment, management, and mitigation, helping organizations protect their information assets and comply with regulatory requirements. ISO/IEC 27001 is widely adopted across industries and provides a clear framework for achieving and maintaining high levels of information security.

✓ **CIS Controls:** The Center for Internet Security (CIS) Controls are a set of best practices designed to help organizations defend against common cybersecurity threats. The controls are organized into three categories: Basic, Foundational, and Organizational. Each category includes a series of specific, actionable recommendations for improving security practices, such as implementing access controls, securing configurations, and monitoring for threats. The CIS Controls provide a practical, prioritized approach to enhancing cybersecurity and are widely used by organizations to build and strengthen their security programs.

✓ **COBIT:** The Control Objectives for Information and Related Technologies (COBIT) framework, developed by ISACA, provides a comprehensive approach to managing and governing enterprise IT. It focuses on aligning IT goals with business objectives and ensuring that IT processes and controls support effective risk management and compliance. COBIT includes a set of guidelines and best practices for IT governance, risk management, and control, helping organizations achieve their strategic goals while maintaining robust security and compliance. The framework is widely used by organizations to improve IT management and ensure that IT resources are effectively utilized and protected.

Best Practice For Cyber Security

Implementing Strong Access Controls

Access control is a fundamental aspect of cybersecurity that involves managing who can access what information within an organization. Implementing strong access controls ensures that only authorized individuals have access to sensitive information and critical systems. This practice begins with a robust authentication process, typically involving multi-factor authentication (MFA) to add an extra layer of security beyond just passwords. Additionally, organizations should enforce the principle of least privilege, granting users only the access necessary to perform their job functions. Regular audits of access rights are also essential to ensure that permissions are up-to-date and appropriate.

Regularly Updating and Patching Systems

Keeping software and systems up-to-date with the latest patches is crucial for protecting against known vulnerabilities. Cyber attackers often exploit security flaws in outdated software to gain unauthorized access or cause disruptions. Organizations should establish a systematic patch management process to ensure timely updates of all software, operating systems, and firmware. This involves monitoring for new vulnerabilities, testing patches in a controlled environment before deployment, and ensuring that patches are applied consistently across all systems.

Conducting Security Awareness Training

Human error is one of the leading causes of security breaches. Therefore, educating employees about cybersecurity best practices is critical. Regular security awareness training helps employees recognize and respond appropriately to potential threats such as phishing attacks, social engineering, and malware. Training should be continuous and updated to reflect the latest threats and tactics used by cybercriminals. By fostering a culture of security awareness, organizations can significantly reduce the risk of successful attacks.

Implementing Network Security Measures

Network security involves protecting the integrity, confidentiality, and availability of data as it is transmitted across networks. Best practices in network security include the use of firewalls to control incoming and outgoing traffic based on predetermined security rules. Intrusion detection and prevention systems (IDPS) can monitor network traffic for suspicious activity and respond to potential threats. Additionally, segmenting the network into smaller, isolated sections can limit the spread of malware and restrict attackers' movement within the network.

Conducting Regular Security Assessments and Penetration Testing

Regular security assessments and penetration testing are essential for identifying and addressing vulnerabilities before they can be exploited by attackers. Security assessments involve a comprehensive review of an organization's security posture, including policies, procedures, and technical controls. Penetration testing, on the other hand, simulates real-world attacks to identify weaknesses that may not be apparent through traditional assessments. These activities should be conducted regularly and after significant changes to the IT environment to ensure ongoing security.

Implementing Data Encryption

Data encryption is the process of converting data into a coded format that can only be read by someone with the appropriate decryption key. Encryption protects data at rest, in transit, and in use, ensuring that even if data is intercepted or accessed without authorization, it remains unreadable. Best practices for data encryption include using strong encryption algorithms, managing encryption keys securely, and ensuring that all sensitive data is encrypted, especially when stored on portable devices or transmitted over unsecured networks.

Developing and Enforcing a Robust Security Policy

A comprehensive security policy is the foundation of an effective cybersecurity program. This policy should outline the organization's approach to managing security, including roles and responsibilities, acceptable use of IT resources, and procedures for incident response. The security policy should be regularly reviewed and updated to reflect changes in the threat landscape and organizational structure. Enforcing the policy through regular training and audits ensures that it is followed consistently throughout the organization.

Implementing Endpoint Protection Solutions

Endpoints, such as laptops, desktops, and mobile devices, are common targets for cyber attacks. Implementing endpoint protection solutions, such as antivirus software, anti-malware tools, and endpoint detection and response (EDR) systems, is essential for safeguarding these devices. These tools provide real-time monitoring and protection against a wide range of threats, including viruses, ransomware, and spyware. Regularly updating endpoint protection solutions ensures they can defend against the latest threats.

Creating a Comprehensive Incident Response Plan

Despite best efforts, security incidents can and do occur. Having a comprehensive incident response plan in place is critical for minimizing the impact of a breach and recovering quickly. This plan should outline the steps to be taken in the event of an incident, including identification, containment, eradication, recovery, and lessons learned. Regular drills and simulations can help ensure that all team members are familiar with the plan and can execute it effectively under pressure.

Ensuring Secure Configuration of Systems

Secure configuration involves setting up systems and software to minimize vulnerabilities. This includes disabling unnecessary services and features, changing default passwords, and configuring security settings according to best practices. Secure configuration is particularly important for internet-facing systems, which are often targeted by attackers. Regularly reviewing and updating configurations ensures they remain secure as new threats emerge and as the organization's IT environment evolves.

Implementing Robust Backup and Recovery Processes

Data loss can occur due to cyber attacks, hardware failures, or other unexpected events. Implementing robust backup and recovery processes ensures that critical data can be restored quickly and accurately in the event of a loss. Best practices include regularly backing up data, storing backups in multiple locations (including offsite or cloud storage), and periodically testing backup and recovery procedures to ensure they work as intended.

Monitoring and Logging Activities

Continuous monitoring and logging of network and system activities are essential for detecting and responding to security incidents. Implementing a security information and event management (SIEM) system can help aggregate and analyze logs from various sources, providing real-time alerts on suspicious activities. Regularly reviewing logs and conducting audits can help identify potential security issues and ensure compliance with security policies and regulations.

By adhering to these best practices, organizations can significantly enhance their cybersecurity posture, protecting their information assets and maintaining the trust of their customers, partners, and stakeholders.

CHAPTER **7**

CYBERSECURITY FOR BUSINESS

Cybersecurity is crucial for businesses of all sizes and sectors due to the increasing prevalence and sophistication of cyber threats. Businesses face a multitude of risks, including data breaches, ransomware attacks, and insider threats, which can lead to significant financial losses, reputational damage, and legal consequences. Protecting sensitive business information, such as customer data, financial records, and intellectual property, is essential for maintaining trust, ensuring regulatory compliance, and sustaining operations. Implementing robust cybersecurity measures is not only a defense against these threats but also a critical component of a comprehensive risk management strategy. A well-rounded cybersecurity strategy for businesses includes a combination of technology, policies, and practices designed to protect against various types of threats. This strategy often involves deploying advanced security technologies such as firewalls, intrusion detection and prevention systems, and endpoint protection solutions. In addition to technological defenses, businesses should establish clear security policies and procedures, including regular employee training and awareness programs. By fostering a security-conscious culture, businesses can help ensure that employees understand their roles in protecting the organization and are equipped to recognize and respond to potential threats.

Risk assessment and management are fundamental aspects of a business's cybersecurity efforts. Conducting regular risk assessments helps identify vulnerabilities and potential threats, allowing businesses to prioritize their security measures based on the level of risk. This process includes evaluating the security of systems, networks, and applications, as well as assessing the effectiveness of existing controls. By understanding the specific risks they face, businesses can develop targeted strategies to mitigate these risks and strengthen their overall security posture.

Data protection is a key focus of cybersecurity for businesses. Ensuring the confidentiality, integrity, and availability of sensitive data requires implementing strong encryption methods, access controls, and data backup procedures. Encryption protects data both in transit and at rest, making it unreadable to unauthorized individuals. Access controls, such as role-based permissions, ensure that only authorized personnel can access sensitive information. Regular data backups are essential for recovery in case of data loss or ransomware attacks, ensuring business continuity and minimizing downtime.

Compliance with industry regulations and standards is also an important consideration for businesses in their cybersecurity efforts. Many industries are subject to specific regulations that mandate certain security practices, such as the General Data Protection Regulation (GDPR) for businesses operating in the European Union or the Health Insurance Portability and Accountability Act (HIPAA) for healthcare organizations in the United States. Adhering to these regulations not only helps businesses avoid legal penalties but also demonstrates a commitment to protecting sensitive information and maintaining high security standards. By integrating compliance requirements into their cybersecurity strategies, businesses can better safeguard their data and build trust with customers and partners.

7.1. Small and Medium-Sized Enterprises (SMEs)

Small and medium-sized enterprises (SMEs) form the backbone of many economies, contributing significantly to employment and economic growth. Despite their critical role, SMEs often face unique challenges when it comes to cybersecurity. Limited resources, both in terms of budget and personnel, can constrain their ability to implement and maintain robust security measures. Unlike larger organizations, SMEs may not have dedicated IT or cybersecurity teams, making it difficult to stay abreast of evolving threats and best practices. This resource limitation can leave SMEs vulnerable to cyber attacks, which can have severe repercussions, including financial losses and damage to their reputation.

One of the key challenges for SMEs is the lack of specialized cybersecurity knowledge and skills. Many SMEs operate with small teams where employees wear multiple hats, including managing IT and security tasks. This can result in a lack of in-depth cybersecurity expertise and awareness. Additionally, SMEs might struggle to provide comprehensive security training to their employees, increasing the risk of human error and susceptibility to cyber threats such as phishing and social engineering attacks. Without dedicated cybersecurity resources, SMEs may find it challenging to develop and implement effective security policies and practices.

To address these challenges, SMEs can adopt cost-effective and scalable cybersecurity solutions. Leveraging cloud-based security services and managed security service providers (MSSPs) can provide advanced protection without requiring significant upfront investments. Implementing fundamental security practices, such as strong password policies, regular software updates, and employee training, can also enhance their security posture. By taking a proactive approach to cybersecurity and focusing on critical areas, SMEs can better protect their assets, ensure business continuity, and mitigate the risks associated with cyber threats.

Specific Challenges and Solutions

1. Limited Resources and Budget Constraints

- ✓ **Challenge:** SMEs often operate with limited budgets and resources, which can significantly impact their ability to invest in robust cybersecurity measures. Unlike large enterprises, SMEs may not have the financial capacity to purchase advanced security technologies or hire dedicated cybersecurity professionals. This constraint can result in inadequate protection against cyber threats and a higher risk of security breaches.

- ✓ **Solution:** SMEs can address this challenge by focusing on costeffective cybersecurity solutions and leveraging available resources strategically. Cloud-based security services and managed security service providers (MSSPs) offer scalable and affordable protection without substantial upfront costs. Additionally, SMEs can prioritize essential security measures, such as firewalls, antivirus software, and regular software updates, to build a solid defense. Implementing free or lowcost security tools, such as basic encryption and access controls, can also help enhance security without significant financial investment.

2. Lack of Cybersecurity Expertise

- ✓ **Challenge:** Many SMEs lack in-house cybersecurity expertise, which can hinder their ability to effectively manage and respond to cyber threats. Small teams or business owners may not have the specialized knowledge required to implement comprehensive security measures or to stay current with evolving threats and best practices. This knowledge gap can leave SMEs vulnerable to attacks and reduce their ability to effectively handle security incidents.

✓ **Solution:** To overcome the lack of expertise, SMEs can seek external support from cybersecurity consultants or MSSPs who offer specialized knowledge and services. These external experts can assist in assessing security needs, implementing best practices, and managing security operations. Additionally, SMEs should invest in training programs for their employees to increase awareness of cybersecurity risks and best practices. This training can help staff recognize and respond to common threats, such as phishing attacks, and reduce the likelihood of human error.

3. Inadequate Incident Response and Recovery Plans

✓ **Challenge:** SMEs may not have well-developed incident response and recovery plans, making it difficult to respond effectively to security breaches. Without a clear plan, SMEs can struggle to contain and mitigate the impact of an attack, leading to prolonged downtime and greater financial losses. The lack of preparedness can also result in poor communication with stakeholders and regulatory bodies.

✓ **Solution:** Developing a comprehensive incident response and recovery plan is essential for SMEs to effectively manage security incidents. This plan should outline procedures for detecting, responding to, and recovering from attacks, as well as communication strategies for informing stakeholders and regulators. SMEs can create a plan by identifying critical assets, establishing response teams, and conducting regular drills to test the effectiveness of their procedures. Engaging with external experts for guidance and support in developing and refining these plans can also enhance preparedness and resilience.

4. Cybersecurity Awareness and Training

✓ **Challenge:** Employees in SMEs may not receive adequate training on cybersecurity best practices, leading to increased susceptibility to threats such as phishing and social engineering. Without a strong understanding of potential risks and proper security behaviors, employees may inadvertently compromise the organization's security.

✓ **Solution:** Implementing regular cybersecurity training programs for employees is crucial for enhancing awareness and reducing risk. Training should cover topics such as recognizing phishing attempts, using strong passwords, and following secure practices for handling sensitive information. Additionally, SMEs should create a culture of security by encouraging open communication about cybersecurity issues and promoting ongoing education. Regular updates and refresher courses can help employees stay informed about new threats and best practices.

5. Compliance with Regulations

✓ **Challenge:** SMEs often face difficulties in navigating and adhering to industry-specific regulations and standards related to data protection and cybersecurity. Compliance can be complex and resource-intensive, especially for smaller organizations with limited legal and technical expertise.

✓ **Solution:** SMEs can address compliance challenges by seeking guidance from legal and cybersecurity experts who specialize in regulatory requirements. Implementing standardized security frameworks and best practices can also help streamline compliance efforts. For example, adopting frameworks such as the NIST Cybersecurity Framework or ISO/IEC 27001 can provide structured guidance on achieving and maintaining compliance. Additionally, SMEs should regularly review and update their security practices to align with changing regulations and industry standards.

7.2. Large Enterprises

Large enterprises often operate on a global scale, managing vast networks and an extensive range of IT systems and applications. This scale and complexity pose unique challenges in maintaining robust cybersecurity. Large organizations typically handle significant volumes of sensitive data, including customer information, financial records, and intellectual property. Securing this data requires sophisticated technology and a well-coordinated security strategy to address the diverse and evolving threats faced by the organization. Ensuring consistent security across numerous departments, locations, and business units demands substantial resources and coordination.

The sheer size and complexity of large enterprises mean that they often have intricate IT environments. This includes a mix of on-premises systems, cloud services, and third-party applications, all of which need to be secured. Managing this diversity requires a comprehensive approach to integrating security measures across various platforms and technologies. Large enterprises must implement a unified security strategy that ensures effective protection across all components of their IT infrastructure. This often involves deploying advanced security technologies, such as unified threat management (UTM) systems, and implementing complex access controls and encryption methods.

Large enterprises also face significant challenges related to managing and securing large teams of IT and security professionals. Coordinating efforts across different regions, business units, and departments requires effective communication and collaboration. Establishing standardized security practices and protocols is essential to ensure that all employees adhere to the same security policies and procedures.

Centralized management of security operations, including regular security assessments and audits, helps maintain a cohesive security posture and address potential vulnerabilities in a timely manner.

Compliance with industry regulations and standards is a critical concern for large enterprises. Many large organizations are subject to strict regulatory requirements, such as the General Data Protection Regulation (GDPR) or the Health Insurance Portability and Accountability Act (HIPAA). Meeting these compliance requirements involves implementing robust security controls, conducting regular audits, and providing detailed documentation of security practices. Ensuring adherence to these regulations is essential not only for avoiding legal penalties but also for maintaining customer trust and protecting sensitive information.

Large enterprises must continuously adapt their security strategies to address emerging threats and technological advancements. This includes investing in cutting-edge security technologies, such as artificial intelligence (AI) and machine learning, to enhance threat detection and response capabilities. Regularly updating security policies, conducting risk assessments, and staying informed about the latest threat trends are crucial for maintaining a strong security posture. By proactively addressing these challenges, large enterprises can better protect their assets, ensure business continuity, and mitigate the risks associated with cyber threats.

Complex Security Architectures

Large enterprises often operate with complex security architectures that encompass a wide range of technologies, systems, and processes. Managing these architectures requires integrating various security solutions and ensuring that they work seamlessly together. This complexity can include multiple layers of security, such as firewalls, intrusion detection systems (IDS), and advanced threat protection, all of which must be configured and maintained effectively. The challenge lies in coordinating these diverse elements to provide comprehensive protection across the entire IT environment.

One key aspect of managing complex security architectures is ensuring consistency and coherence across different components. Large enterprises often use a combination of on-premises systems and cloud services, each with its own security requirements. Integrating security measures across these environments requires careful planning and implementation. For example, ensuring that cloud-based security controls align with on-premises security policies can be challenging but is essential for maintaining a unified security posture. Additionally, managing security across various third-party applications and services adds another layer of complexity.

Another challenge is maintaining visibility and control over the entire security landscape. With numerous security tools and technologies in place, it can be difficult to obtain a comprehensive view of the organization's security status. Centralized security management solutions, such as Security Information and Event Management (SIEM) systems, can help aggregate and analyze data from various sources to provide a holistic view of the security environment. These tools enable organizations to monitor security events in real-time, identify potential threats, and respond promptly to incidents.

The complexity of security architectures also necessitates ongoing maintenance and updates to address evolving threats. As new vulnerabilities and attack vectors emerge, organizations must continuously update their security solutions and policies. This includes deploying patches, configuring new security features, and adapting to changes in the threat landscape. Regular security assessments and audits are crucial for identifying potential weaknesses and ensuring that security measures remain effective against emerging threats.

Effective management of complex security architectures requires a welldefined strategy and strong coordination among IT and security teams. Establishing clear roles and responsibilities, implementing standardized procedures, and fostering collaboration between different departments are essential for maintaining a cohesive security posture. By addressing these challenges and focusing on integrated, adaptive security solutions, large enterprises can better protect their assets and ensure a resilient security environment.

7.3. Supply chain security

Supply chain security is a critical aspect of overall cybersecurity strategy, especially as organizations increasingly rely on third-party vendors and partners for various services and products. The interconnected nature of modern supply chains means that vulnerabilities or breaches within a supplier's system can have a cascading impact on the entire network. Ensuring that each link in the supply chain is secure is essential for protecting sensitive information and maintaining the integrity of business operations. Given that suppliers may handle critical data or access key systems, their security practices directly affect the organization's overall risk profile.

One of the primary challenges in supply chain security is assessing and managing the security posture of third-party vendors. Organizations often lack visibility into the security controls and practices of their suppliers, making it difficult to evaluate potential risks. Vendors may have varying levels of security maturity and could introduce vulnerabilities if their systems are not adequately protected. To address this, organizations need to implement comprehensive third-party risk management programs that include detailed assessments of vendor security practices, regular security audits, and ongoing monitoring. Establishing clear security requirements in contracts and agreements can also help ensure that suppliers meet the organization's security standards.

Developing robust incident response plans that address supply chain security is crucial for managing potential risks. Organizations should have procedures in place for identifying, containing, and mitigating the impact of security incidents involving third-party vendors. This includes defining communication protocols, coordinating with affected suppliers, and implementing remediation steps. By preparing for potential breaches and establishing strong relationships with suppliers, organizations can enhance their ability to respond effectively to security incidents and minimize disruptions to their operations. Effective supply chain security requires continuous vigilance, collaboration, and adaptation to evolving threats and challenges.

Managing Third-Party Risks

Managing third-party risks is a crucial component of an organization's overall risk management strategy, given the reliance on external vendors and partners for various services and products. Third-party risks encompass a range of potential threats arising from interactions with suppliers, contractors, and other external entities that have access to an organization's systems or data. These risks include security vulnerabilities, compliance issues, and potential disruptions to business operations. Effective management of third-party risks involves a systematic approach to assessing, monitoring, and mitigating these risks throughout the lifecycle of the third-party relationship.

1. **Risk Assessment and Due Diligence:** The first step in managing third-party risks is conducting a thorough risk assessment and due diligence before engaging with a new vendor. This process involves evaluating the security posture and practices of potential third parties to identify any vulnerabilities or weaknesses that could impact the organization. Key areas of assessment include the vendor's security policies, data protection measures, and compliance with relevant regulations and standards. Organizations should request and review security documentation, perform background checks, and, if necessary, conduct on-site assessments. By understanding the potential risks associated with a third-party, organizations

can make informed decisions and establish appropriate security requirements and controls.

2. **Contractual Agreements and Security Requirements:** Once a third-party relationship is established, it is essential to formalize security expectations and requirements through contractual agreements. Contracts should include specific clauses that outline the vendor's obligations related to data protection, security controls, and compliance with relevant regulations. This may include requirements for regular security audits, incident reporting, and remediation procedures. Clearly defined roles and responsibilities, along with agreed-upon service level agreements (SLAs), help ensure that both parties understand their obligations and can address any issues that arise promptly. Contracts should also address the process for managing changes to the vendor's security environment and handling potential breaches or security incidents.

3. **Continuous Monitoring and Performance Evaluation:** Managing third-party risks is an ongoing process that requires continuous monitoring and performance evaluation. Organizations should regularly review and assess the security practices of their vendors to ensure ongoing compliance with contractual agreements and security requirements. This can include periodic security audits, vulnerability assessments, and performance reviews. Additionally, monitoring should extend to assessing the vendor's overall risk management practices, including their response to emerging threats and changes in their security environment. By maintaining visibility into the vendor's security posture, organizations can identify potential issues early and take proactive steps to address them.

4. **Incident Response and Remediation:** An effective incident response plan is critical for managing third-party risks and addressing security incidents involving vendors. The plan should

outline procedures for detecting, containing, and mitigating the impact of a security breach or vulnerability associated with a third party. It should also include communication protocols for notifying stakeholders, regulators, and affected parties. Coordination with the vendor is essential for managing the incident and implementing remediation measures. Organizations should work closely with their vendors to understand the root cause of the incident, apply necessary fixes, and prevent future occurrences. Post-incident reviews and lessons learned can help improve the organization's overall approach to thirdparty risk management.

5. **Building Strong Relationships and Collaboration:** Building strong relationships with third-party vendors can enhance the effectiveness of risk management efforts. Establishing open lines of communication and fostering collaboration can help address potential security issues more effectively and ensure that both parties are aligned on security goals and practices. Regular meetings and information sharing can help build trust and facilitate a proactive approach to managing risks. By working together, organizations and their vendors can better understand each other's security needs and requirements, leading to a more resilient and secure supply chain.

By addressing these aspects, organizations can better protect their assets, ensure compliance, and maintain a robust security posture in the face of evolving threats and challenges.

CHAPTER

8

LEGAL AND ETHICAL ASPECTS

Cybersecurity encompasses both legal and ethical dimensions that are essential for ensuring responsible and compliant practices in protecting information systems and data. From a legal standpoint, organizations must adhere to a range of laws and regulations designed to safeguard personal and sensitive information. These laws often mandate specific security measures, data protection protocols, and reporting requirements. Non-compliance with these regulations can lead to significant legal penalties, including fines and legal action. Moreover, legal obligations may vary by jurisdiction, requiring organizations to stay informed about and adhere to relevant laws in the regions where they operate.

Ethically, cybersecurity professionals and organizations are expected to uphold principles of integrity, transparency, and respect for privacy. Ethical considerations involve making decisions that prioritize the protection of individual privacy and ensure that security measures do not infringe on personal freedoms. For instance, while monitoring network activity is necessary for security, it must be balanced with respect for employees' privacy rights. Ethical hacking practices, such as those performed by white hat hackers, should be conducted with explicit permission and in a manner that aims to improve security rather than exploit vulnerabilities for personal gain.

Legal and ethical responsibilities also intersect in the realm of data breaches and incident response. Organizations are legally required to notify affected individuals and authorities in the event of a data breach, but they must also handle these situations ethically. This means providing clear and honest communication about the breach, its potential impact, and the steps being taken to address the issue. Ethical incident management involves taking responsibility, providing support to affected individuals, and implementing measures to prevent future breaches.

Additionally, the ethical implications of cybersecurity extend to the development and implementation of security technologies. Developers and organizations must consider how their technologies could be used or misused. This includes ensuring that security tools and systems do not inadvertently contribute to harmful activities or violate users' rights. Ethical considerations should guide the design and deployment of cybersecurity solutions to ensure they serve the intended purpose without unintended negative consequences.

Finally, the legal and ethical aspects of cybersecurity require ongoing education and awareness. As technology evolves and new threats emerge, both legal requirements and ethical standards may change. Cybersecurity professionals and organizations must stay informed about legal developments and ethical best practices to ensure compliance and uphold high standards of integrity. Continuous training and awareness programs can help address these dynamic aspects of cybersecurity, fostering a culture of responsibility and adherence to both legal and ethical standards.

8.1. Cyber Laws and Regulations

The General Data Protection Regulation (GDPR) is a comprehensive data protection regulation enacted by the European Union, which came into effect on May 25, 2018. GDPR aims to protect the personal data and privacy of EU citizens and residents. It establishes strict guidelines on how organizations collect, process, store, and share personal data. GDPR requires organizations to obtain explicit consent from individuals before processing their data and mandates the implementation of robust data security measures. It also grants individuals the right to access their data, request corrections, and demand deletion. Noncompliance with GDPR can result in substantial fines, making it crucial for organizations operating in or dealing with EU residents to adhere to its requirements.

The California Consumer Privacy Act (CCPA), effective from January 1, 2020, is a significant privacy law in the United States that focuses on the protection of personal information for California residents. CCPA provides consumers with the right to know what personal information is being collected about them, to access and delete that information, and to opt out of its sale. It also imposes obligations on businesses to disclose their data collection practices and to implement reasonable security measures to protect personal information. The CCPA applies to businesses that meet certain criteria, including those that have significant revenues or handle a large volume of personal data.

Compliance with CCPA is essential for businesses operating in California or engaging with California residents.

8.2. Ethical Hacking

Ethical hacking involves the practice of authorized and legal hacking activities to identify and address security vulnerabilities in systems and applications. Ethical hackers, also known as white hat hackers, use their skills to conduct penetration testing and vulnerability assessments with the goal of improving security. They operate under explicit permission from the organization they are testing, and their activities are guided by a code of conduct that emphasizes transparency, legality, and respect for privacy. By simulating cyber attacks, ethical hackers help organizations uncover weaknesses and implement necessary security measures to protect against malicious threats.

In contrast, black hat hackers engage in illegal and unauthorized hacking activities for personal gain or malicious intent. Black hat hackers exploit vulnerabilities to steal data, disrupt services, or cause harm to individuals or organizations. Their actions are driven by objectives such as financial gain, political motives, or personal vendettas, and they operate without consent or regard for the ethical implications of their actions. The distinction between white hat and black hat hackers highlights the importance of ethical considerations in cybersecurity and underscores the need for legal and responsible conduct in protecting information systems.

Penetration testing is a key component of ethical hacking, involving simulated attacks on systems to evaluate their security. During a penetration test, ethical hackers use various techniques to identify and exploit vulnerabilities, assessing the effectiveness of existing security measures. The findings from these tests are used to develop strategies for enhancing security and mitigating risks. Penetration testing can be conducted on network systems, web applications, and other digital assets, providing valuable insights into potential weaknesses and helping organizations strengthen their defenses against real-world cyber threats.

CHAPTER

9

CYBERSECURITY IN DIFFERENT SECTORS

Cybersecurity requirements and challenges vary significantly across different sectors due to the unique nature of their operations and the types of data they handle. In the healthcare sector, for instance, protecting patient data is paramount due to the sensitivity and confidentiality of medical records. Health-care organizations must comply with regulations such as the Health Insurance Portability and Accountability Act (HIPAA) in the United States, which mandates strict data protection measures. The sector faces challenges such as safeguarding against ransomware attacks that target patient data, ensuring secure electronic health record (EHR) systems, and addressing vulnerabilities in medical devices that could be exploited by malicious actors.

In the financial sector, cybersecurity is critical to protect sensitive financial information and maintain the integrity of transactions. Financial institutions, including banks and investment firms, handle large volumes of personal and transactional data, making them prime targets for cyber attacks. They must implement robust security measures to prevent data breaches, fraud, and unauthorized access to financial systems. This involves deploying advanced encryption techniques, multi-factor authentication, and continuous monitoring to detect and respond to threats. Regulatory frameworks such as the Payment Card Industry Data Security Standard (PCI DSS) also guide the financial sector in securing payment card transactions and protecting customer information.

The energy sector faces unique cybersecurity challenges due to the critical infrastructure and operational technology it manages. Energy companies, including those involved in electricity generation, oil, and gas, rely on complex systems for controlling and monitoring energy production and distribution. Cyber attacks on these systems can have significant consequences, potentially disrupting supply chains, damaging infrastructure, or causing environmental harm. Ensuring the security of industrial control systems (ICS) and supervisory control and data acquisition (SCADA) systems is crucial for protecting against cyber threats. The sector must also address vulnerabilities associated with the integration of digital technologies and IoT devices in its infrastructure, necessitating a comprehensive approach to cybersecurity that includes both IT and operational technology (OT) security measures.

9.1. Role of Cybersecurity in Different Sectors

1. **Health care:** In the healthcare sector, cybersecurity is crucial for protecting patient data, ensuring privacy, and maintaining trust. The sector handles highly sensitive information, including personal health records and financial details, which are prime targets for cybercriminals. Effective cybersecurity measures are essential to guard against data breaches, ransomware attacks, and unauthorized access to Electronic Health Records (EHRs). Health care organizations must comply with regulations like HIPAA, which require stringent data protection and reporting standards. Cybersecurity efforts also extend to securing medical

devices and systems that could be vulnerable to attacks, ensuring that patient care and safety are not compromised.

2. **Financial Services:** The financial services sector deals with vast amounts of sensitive financial data, including personal banking information, transaction records, and investment details. Cybersecurity in this sector is critical to prevent data breaches, fraud, and theft. Financial institutions must implement advanced security measures such as encryption, multi-factor authentication, and real-time fraud detection systems to protect customer information and financial transactions. Regulatory frameworks like PCI DSS guide the protection of payment card data, while compliance with laws such as the General Data Protection Regulation (GDPR) ensures the secure handling of personal data. The sector also focuses on defending against sophisticated cyber attacks targeting online banking platforms and financial trading systems.

3. **Energy and Utilities:** In the energy and utilities sector, cybersecurity is vital to protect critical infrastructure and ensure the reliable operation of energy systems. This sector manages essential services such as electricity generation, oil and gas production, and water supply, which are increasingly integrated with digital technologies. Cybersecurity measures are necessary to safeguard Industrial Control Systems (ICS) and Supervisory Control and Data Acquisition (SCADA) systems from cyber threats that could disrupt operations or cause physical damage. The sector must also address vulnerabilities associated with the Internet of Things (IoT) devices and ensure the resilience of infrastructure against potential attacks that could impact public safety and environmental stability.

4. **Government and Public Sector:** Cybersecurity in the government and public sector is crucial for protecting sensitive data, maintaining national security, and ensuring the continuity

of public services. Government agencies handle classified information, personal data of citizens, and critical infrastructure details that are attractive targets for cyber espionage and attacks. Robust cybersecurity measures are needed to defend against cyber threats, including data breaches, ransomware attacks, and unauthorized access. The sector must also comply with various regulations and standards related to data protection and cybersecurity, such as the Federal Information Security Management Act (FISMA) in the United States, and work to safeguard the integrity of public services and national security interests.

5. **Education:** In the education sector, cybersecurity is important for protecting student, faculty, and administrative data from breaches and unauthorized access. Educational institutions handle a range of sensitive information, including academic records, financial aid details, and personal data. Cybersecurity measures are necessary to prevent data breaches, phishing attacks, and unauthorized access to educational platforms and research databases. Institutions must implement strong security protocols to protect against cyber threats, ensure the privacy of individuals, and maintain the integrity of academic and administrative systems. As educational institutions increasingly adopt digital tools and online learning platforms, cybersecurity becomes integral to safeguarding educational data and ensuring a safe online environment for students and staff.

9.2. How to get best of Cybersecurity

To get the best out of cybersecurity in your business, you need a comprehensive approach that integrates technology, policies, and practices to effectively protect your assets and data. *Here's a step-bystep guide to optimizing cybersecurity for your business:*

1. Conduct a Risk Assessment

Begin by identifying and assessing the specific risks and vulnerabilities that your business faces. This includes understanding the types of data you handle, the potential threats, and the impact of a security breach. Conduct a thorough risk assessment to determine which areas require the most attention and which security measures are necessary to mitigate those risks.

2. Develop a Cybersecurity Strategy

Create a robust cybersecurity strategy that outlines your security goals, policies, and procedures. This strategy should include risk management practices, incident response plans, and guidelines for maintaining data privacy and security. Your strategy should also align with industry best practices and regulatory requirements relevant to your business.

3. Implement Strong Security Measures

Deploy a range of security technologies and solutions to protect your business. This includes:

- ✓ **Firewalls:** To block unauthorized access and monitor incoming and outgoing traffic.

- ✓ **Antivirus Software:** To detect and remove malware and other malicious software.

- ✓ **Encryption:** To protect sensitive data both in transit and at rest.

- ✓ **Multi-Factor Authentication (MFA):** To add an extra layer of security for user access.

4. Educate and Train Employees

Human error is often the weakest link in cybersecurity. Regularly train your employees on cybersecurity best practices, such as recognizing phishing attempts, creating strong passwords, and following data protection protocols. Conduct ongoing awareness programs to keep staff informed about emerging threats and safe practices.

5. Monitor and Respond

Implement continuous monitoring solutions to detect and respond to security incidents in real time. This includes setting up intrusion detection systems (IDS) and intrusion prevention systems (IPS) to identify and mitigate threats. Develop a clear incident response plan that outlines the steps to take if a breach occurs, including communication protocols, containment strategies, and recovery procedures.

6. Regularly Update and Patch Systems

Keep all software, hardware, and systems up to date with the latest security patches and updates. Regularly updating and patching systems helps protect against known vulnerabilities and exploits that could be used by attackers.

7. Backup Critical Data

Regularly back up critical data and ensure that backups are stored securely. Implement a backup strategy that includes both on site and offsite backups to ensure that data can be recovered in the event of a disaster or cyber attack.

8. Implement Access Controls

Use access control mechanisms to ensure that only authorized personnel can access sensitive information and systems. Implement role-based access controls (RBAC) to limit access based on job responsibilities and ensure that permissions are regularly reviewed and updated.

9. Conduct Regular Security Audits

Perform regular security audits and assessments to evaluate the effectiveness of your cybersecurity measures. Engage third-party experts to conduct penetration testing and vulnerability assessments to identify potential weaknesses and areas for improvement.

10. Stay Informed and Adapt

Cybersecurity is an evolving field with new threats and technologies emerging regularly. Stay informed about the latest cybersecurity trends, threats, and best practices. Continuously adapt your security strategy and measures to address new challenges and improve your overall security posture.

By following these steps, you can enhance your business's cybersecurity defenses, protect your data, and reduce the risk of cyber attacks. Implementing a proactive and comprehensive approach will help ensure that your business is well-equipped to handle the evolving threat landscape.

CHAPTER

10

THE FUTURE OF CYBERSECURITY

The future of cybersecurity is poised to be shaped by a rapidly evolving technological landscape and the increasing sophistication of cyber threats. As organizations continue to adopt advanced technologies such as artificial intelligence (AI), the Internet of Things (IoT), and cloud computing, the complexity and volume of potential vulnerabilities will rise. AI and machine learning will play a dual role, both enhancing cybersecurity defenses through advanced threat detection and predictive analytics and potentially being exploited by cybercriminals for sophisticated attacks. The integration of AI-driven security solutions will enable more proactive threat management, allowing for real-time response and adaptive security measures. However, this also necessitates a focus on ensuring that AI systems themselves are secure and free from biases that could compromise their effectiveness.

The growing reliance on cloud computing will also significantly impact the future of cybersecurity. Cloud environments offer scalability and flexibility but come with their own set of security challenges, including data breaches, misconfigured settings, and vulnerabilities in cloud service providers' infrastructure. As businesses increasingly migrate to cloud platforms, securing cloud environments will become paramount. This includes adopting robust cloud security practices such as data encryption, identity and access management, and continuous monitoring. Additionally, the rise of hybrid and multi-cloud environments will require integrated security solutions that provide consistent protection across diverse cloud infrastructures.

The proliferation of IoT devices presents both opportunities and risks for cybersecurity. IoT devices, which include everything from smart home gadgets to industrial sensors, expand the attack surface of networks and systems. Many IoT devices lack built-in security features and may be vulnerable to exploitation. The future of cybersecurity will involve developing and implementing standards and protocols to secure IoT devices and ensure that they are resistant to attacks. This will also require greater collaboration between device manufacturers, security experts, and regulatory bodies to establish comprehensive security frameworks and practices for IoT ecosystems.

Finally, the evolving regulatory landscape and increasing focus on data privacy will shape the future of cybersecurity. Governments and regulatory bodies are expected to introduce more stringent regulations to protect personal data and ensure compliance with privacy standards. Organizations will need to navigate a complex web of regulations, including data protection laws like GDPR and CCPA, and adapt their cybersecurity strategies accordingly. This will drive a greater emphasis on transparency, data governance, and accountability in cybersecurity practices. As privacy concerns grow, businesses will be required to prioritize the protection of personal information and implement measures that align with both legal requirements and ethical considerations.

Organizations must stay ahead of these developments by adopting cutting-edge security technologies, addressing new vulnerabilities, and ensuring compliance with emerging regulations to effectively safeguard their assets and data.

10.1. Emerging Threats

Emerging threats in the future of cybersecurity are expected to evolve alongside advancements in technology, presenting new challenges for organizations and individuals alike. One significant concern is the rise of quantum computing, which has the potential to break current encryption methods and undermine the security of encrypted data. As quantum technology progresses, it may enable attackers to solve complex cryptographic problems much faster than traditional computers, necessitating the development of quantum-resistant encryption algorithms to safeguard sensitive information. Additionally, the increasing integration of Internet of Things (IoT) devices into daily life expands the attack surface, as many of these devices lack robust security features and can be exploited to launch attacks or gather data. Another emerging threat is the use of artificial intelligence (AI) and machine learning by cybercriminals to automate and enhance their attacks. AI-driven tools can analyze vast amounts of data to identify vulnerabilities, craft sophisticated phishing schemes, and even execute targeted cyberattacks with precision. The potential for AI to be used in deepfakes and misinformation campaigns also poses significant risks, as attackers could manipulate public perception or deceive individuals and organizations. As these technologies advance, it will be crucial to develop and implement advanced defensive measures, including AIpowered security solutions and comprehensive strategies to address the evolving threat landscape. *Other emerging threats are as follow:*

✓ **AI and Machine Learning in Cyber Attacks**

Artificial Intelligence (AI) and machine learning (ML) are rapidly advancing technologies with the potential to both enhance and undermine cybersecurity. In the realm of cyber attacks, malicious actors are increasingly leveraging AI and ML to develop more sophisticated and adaptive threats. AI-powered tools can automate and accelerate the process of discovering vulnerabilities and crafting phishing attacks, making them more convincing and difficult to detect. Machine learning algorithms can analyze vast amounts of data to identify patterns and anomalies, enabling attackers to execute more precise and targeted attacks. These technologies can also facilitate the creation of advanced malware that can adapt and evolve in response to defensive measures, complicating efforts to detect and neutralize such threats.

Conversely, AI and machine learning offer significant advantages in defending against cyber threats. Security systems equipped with AI can enhance threat detection by analyzing patterns and behaviors at a scale and speed beyond human capability. Machine learning models can improve over time, becoming more effective at identifying new types of attacks and reducing false positives. However, the dual-use nature of these technologies means that while they provide powerful tools for defenders, they also arm attackers with advanced capabilities. This escalating arms race between offensive and defensive applications of AI and ML underscores the need for continuous innovation and adaptation in cybersecurity practices.

✓ **Quantum Computing and Its Impact**

Quantum computing represents a transformative leap in computational power, but it also poses significant risks to current cryptographic standards. Unlike classical computers, which process information in binary bits, quantum computers use quantum bits (qubits) to perform complex calculations at unprecedented speeds. This capability could potentially render current encryption algorithms obsolete, as quantum computers might be able to break encryption methods that are currently considered secure, such as RSA and ECC. The ability of quantum computers to solve complex mathematical problems quickly could lead to the decryption of sensitive data, posing a grave threat to information security and requiring the development of quantumresistant encryption algorithms to protect against future breaches.

In response to the threat posed by quantum computing, researchers and cybersecurity professionals are already working on post-quantum cryptography—encryption methods designed to be secure against quantum attacks. This involves developing new cryptographic algorithms that can withstand the computational power of quantum computers. Transitioning to these new standards will be a complex and time-consuming process, necessitating collaboration across the cybersecurity industry and government bodies. As quantum computing technology continues to advance, preparing for its impact will be crucial to maintaining the integrity of data security and ensuring that protective measures evolve in tandem with technological developments.

10.2. Trends and Innovations in Cybersecurity

1. **The Rise of Zero Trust Architecture:** One of the most significant trends in cybersecurity is the adoption of Zero Trust Architecture (ZTA), which fundamentally shifts the traditional security model. Instead of relying on perimeter defenses to protect the network, Zero Trust operates on the principle of "never trust, always verify." This approach requires continuous authentication and authorization for every user and device, regardless of their location. By implementing strict access controls and monitoring all network traffic, Zero Trust minimizes the risk of insider threats and breaches that bypass perimeter defenses. Innovations in identity and access management (IAM), micro-segmentation, and behavioral analytics are key components of this approach, helping

organizations to better secure their systems and data in an increasingly complex and distributed IT environment.

2. **Integration of Artificial Intelligence and Machine Learning:** Artificial Intelligence (AI) and Machine Learning (ML) are becoming integral to cybersecurity, offering advanced capabilities for threat detection and response. AI and ML algorithms can analyze large volumes of data to identify patterns and anomalies that may indicate potential threats. These technologies enable the development of intelligent security systems that can adapt to evolving attack vectors and automate responses to detected threats. For example, AI-driven Security Information and Event Management (SIEM) systems can provide real-time analysis and incident response, reducing the time it takes to detect and mitigate attacks. Innovations in AI and ML are enhancing the ability of security teams to preemptively address vulnerabilities and respond more effectively to sophisticated cyber threats.

3. **Expansion of Cloud Security Solutions:** As organizations increasingly migrate to cloud environments, cloud security has become a critical focus. Cloud security solutions are evolving to address the unique challenges associated with cloud computing, such as data breaches, misconfigurations, and insecure interfaces. Innovations in this area include advanced encryption techniques, secure access controls, and cloud-native security tools that provide visibility and control over cloud resources. The development of Cloud Access Security Brokers (CASBs) and cloud security posture management (CSPM) tools helps organizations enforce security policies and ensure compliance with regulatory requirements. As cloud adoption grows, securing cloud environments remains a priority, with ongoing advancements aimed at enhancing protection and managing risk in multi-cloud and hybrid cloud scenarios.

4. **Increased Emphasis on Privacy and Data Protection:** Privacy and data protection are becoming central to cybersecurity strategies due to growing regulatory requirements and consumer expectations. The implementation of data protection laws such as the General Data Protection Regulation (GDPR) and the California Consumer Privacy Act (CCPA) has heightened the need for organizations to safeguard personal information and ensure compliance. Innovations in data protection include the development of advanced encryption methods, data loss prevention (DLP) technologies, and privacy-enhancing technologies (PETs) that help manage and secure sensitive information. Organizations are also adopting privacy by design principles, integrating data protection measures into the development lifecycle of their products and services to enhance overall security and maintain trust with customers.

5. **Advancements in Security Automation and Orchestration:** Security automation and orchestration are transforming how organizations manage and respond to cybersecurity incidents. By automating routine security tasks and integrating various security tools and systems, organizations can streamline their security operations and improve efficiency. Security Orchestration, Automation, and Response (SOAR) platforms enable automated workflows for threat detection, incident response, and compliance reporting, reducing the manual effort required from security teams. Innovations in this area include the use of orchestration tools to coordinate responses across disparate security solutions and the development of automated threat intelligence sharing systems. As the volume and complexity of cyber threats continue to grow, automation and orchestration are becoming essential for maintaining an effective and agile security posture.

These trends and innovations are shaping the future of cybersecurity, driving advancements in technology and strategies to address emerging threats and protect critical assets. By staying informed and adapting to these changes, organizations can enhance their security posture and better safeguard their digital environments.

10.3. Preparing for the Future in Cybersecurity

1. **Embracing a Proactive Security Posture:** Preparing for the future in cybersecurity requires a shift from reactive to proactive security measures. Organizations must anticipate potential threats and vulnerabilities rather than merely responding to incidents as they occur. This proactive approach involves continuous monitoring and assessment of the security landscape, including emerging threats and technological advancements. Implementing a riskbased strategy that prioritizes critical assets and addresses the most significant risks can help organizations stay ahead of adversaries. Regularly updating and testing incident response plans, conducting threat simulations, and engaging in threat hunting activities are key components of a proactive security posture.

2. **Investing in Emerging Technologies:** To effectively prepare for future cybersecurity challenges, organizations should invest in emerging technologies that enhance their security capabilities. Technologies such as Artificial Intelligence (AI) and Machine Learning (ML) are becoming increasingly important for threat detection, response automation, and vulnerability management. Investing in these technologies can provide advanced analytics, improve threat intelligence, and enable faster response to incidents. Additionally, exploring innovations in quantum-resistant cryptography and cloud security solutions will be crucial as technology evolves and new threats emerge. Staying informed about technological advancements and integrating relevant innovations into security strategies will help organizations maintain robust defenses.

3. **Fostering a Culture of Cybersecurity Awareness:** A critical aspect of preparing for the future is fostering a culture of cybersecurity awareness across the organization. Employees are often the first line of defense against cyber threats, and their awareness and behavior play a significant role in overall security. Implementing ongoing training programs that cover cybersecurity best practices, threat awareness, and safe digital habits can help employees recognize and respond to potential threats. Promoting a security-first mindset and encouraging reporting of suspicious activities can further strengthen the organization's defense. By embedding cybersecurity awareness into the organizational culture, businesses can enhance their resilience to social engineering attacks and other human-centric threats.

4. **Strengthening Collaboration and Partnerships:** Collaboration and partnerships are essential for effectively preparing for future cybersecurity challenges. Cyber threats are increasingly sophisticated and global, requiring a collaborative approach to address them effectively. Organizations should engage with industry peers, government agencies, and cybersecurity experts to share threat intelligence, best practices, and resources. Participating in information-sharing initiatives and joining cybersecurity communities can provide valuable insights and support. Additionally, working with third-party security providers and consultants can help organizations access specialized expertise and technologies that may be beyond their internal capabilities. Strengthening these collaborations can enhance the overall security posture and facilitate a collective response to emerging threats. **5. Adapting to Evolving Regulations and Standards:** As the regulatory landscape for cybersecurity continues to evolve, organizations must stay compliant with new and updated laws and standards. Preparing for the future involves staying informed about changes in cybersecurity regulations, such as the General Data Protection

Regulation (GDPR) and the California Consumer Privacy Act (CCPA), and understanding how they impact the organization. Implementing and maintaining compliance with these regulations not only helps avoid legal penalties but also strengthens data protection and privacy practices. Adapting to evolving standards and frameworks, such as the NIST Cybersecurity Framework or ISO/IEC 27001, ensures that security practices are aligned with industry best practices and regulatory requirements. By proactively addressing compliance issues, organizations can better protect their data and maintain trust with customers and stakeholders. Preparing for the future in cybersecurity involves adopting a proactive security posture, investing in emerging technologies, fostering a culture of awareness, strengthening collaborations, and adapting to evolving regulations. By addressing these key areas, organizations can enhance their ability to anticipate and respond to future cybersecurity challenges, ensuring a resilient and secure digital environment.

CONCLUSION

As we conclude this comprehensive guide to cybersecurity, it is clear that the digital landscape continues to evolve at an unprecedented pace, presenting both opportunities and challenges. Cybersecurity has become a critical component in safeguarding our personal lives, businesses, and national security. The necessity to protect our digital assets from a myriad of cyber threats is more pressing than ever. This book has aimed to provide a thorough understanding of cybersecurity, covering the essentials, exploring various threats, discussing robust prevention techniques, and examining the legal, ethical, and sectorspecific nuances of this vital field.

Throughout this book, we have delved into the fundamentals of cybersecurity, establishing a foundation for understanding its importance and scope. We have examined various types of cyber threats, including malware, phishing, DDoS attacks, and advanced persistent threats, providing insights into how these threats operate and their potential impact. Understanding cyber attack vectors and the methodologies behind network-based, application-based, and physical attacks has highlighted the complexity and multifaceted nature of cyber threats.

Threat detection and prevention techniques have been explored in depth, emphasizing the importance of early detection and the use of advanced tools and methodologies to mitigate risks. The discussion on security frameworks and standards underscored the necessity for structured and compliant approaches to cybersecurity, while best practices provided practical guidance for creating resilient security postures.

Cybersecurity strategies tailored for businesses of all sizes, from SMEs to large enterprises, along with the crucial aspect of supply chain security, have illustrated the varied challenges and solutions across different organizational contexts. Advanced topics such as cryptography, cloud security, and IoT security have showcased the technological advancements and their implications for cybersecurity.

The significance of cybersecurity extends beyond mere protection of data; it encompasses the integrity and trust that underpin our digital society. As cyber threats become more sophisticated, the need for comprehensive and adaptive cybersecurity measures becomes paramount. The evolving regulatory landscape, with laws like GDPR and CCPA, reflects the growing recognition of the importance of data protection and privacy. Ethical hacking and penetration testing highlight the proactive measures required to identify and rectify vulnerabilities before they can be exploited by malicious actors.

At the end of it, cybersecurity is an ongoing journey rather than a destination. The dynamic nature of technology and cyber threats demands continuous learning, adaptation, and vigilance. Organizations and individuals must stay informed about the latest trends, threats, and innovations in cybersecurity to effectively protect their digital environments. Building a culture of cybersecurity awareness, investing in emerging technologies, and fostering collaboration across sectors are essential steps toward achieving robust and resilient cybersecurity defenses.

This book serves as a foundational guide, but the journey does not end here. Readers are encouraged to explore further, stay updated with the latest developments, and actively participate in the collective effort to secure our digital world. By adopting proactive security measures, adhering to best practices, and maintaining a commitment to continuous improvement, we can navigate the complexities of the digital age and safeguard our future.

As we move forward, let us remember that cybersecurity is a shared responsibility. Whether you are an individual, a business, or a government entity, your actions contribute to the collective security of our digital ecosystem. Stay vigilant, stay informed, and stay committed to protecting our digital future.